From Lena Wallis.
December
D1114983

THE LEGACY OF ENGLAND

WALTHAM CROSS, ESSEX

From a Water Colour by
J. M. W. TURNER, R.A.

THE LEGACY OF ENGLAND

AN ILLUSTRATED SURVEY OF THE WORKS OF MAN IN THE ENGLISH COUNTRY

With Contributions by

Adrian Bell, George A. Birmingham, Edmund Blunden, Ivor Brown, Bernard Darwin, Charles Bradley Ford, R. H. Mottram, G. M. Young

and 114 Illustrations from Photographs

LONDON
B. T. BATSFORD LTD
15 NORTH AUDLEY STREET, W.1

First Published, November 1935

MADE AND PRINTED IN GREAT BRITAIN
FOR THE PUBLISHERS, B. T. BATSFORD LTD., LONDON
BY JARROLD AND SONS LTD. NORWICH

CONTENTS

ACKNOWLEDGMENT

THE Publishers must acknowledge their obligation to the photographers whose work is reproduced in these pages, namely, Messrs. Aerofilms, Ltd., for Fig. 59; the late Mr. B. C. Clayton, for Figs. 4, 21, 46; Mr. J. Dixon-Scott, for Figs. 2, 9, 10, 16, 17, 25, 26, 27, 28, 30, 33, 37, 45, 47, 65, 68, 69, 71, 72, 74, 77, 83, 94, 95, 98, 107; Mr. Herbert Felton, for Figs. 5, 8, 39, 40, 66, 85, 99; Fox Photos, for Figs. 11, 111, 112, 114; Mr. F. A. Girling, for Figs. 6, 23, 24, 89, 91; Mr. S. H. Holland, for Fig. 64; Keystone View Co., for Fig. 73; Sport and General, for Figs. 106, 113; Mr. Will F. Taylor, for Figs. 3, 7, 12, 13, 14, 15, 18, 19, 20, 22, 29, 31, 32, 34, 35, 36, 38, 41, 42, 43, 44, 48, 49, 50, 51, 52, 53, 54, 55, 56, 57, 58, 60, 61, 62, 63, 67, 70, 75, 76, 78, 79, 80, 81, 82, 84, 86, 87, 88, 90, 92, 93, 96, 97, 100, 101, 102, 103, 104, 105; Topical Press, for Figs. 108, 109, 110, 115.

FOREWORD

THIS 'Survey of the Works of Man in the English Country' is designed as a companion volume to *The Beauty of Britain*, published last Spring in the same Series, which was received generally with approval by the Press and the public. The object of that work was to form a pictorial survey of the range of unspoilt scenery still to be found in this island; to show how each district is stamped with an individual die and, despite the petrol station and the arterial road, what great riches remain to us of our landscape heritage. It was conspicuous how the majority of contributors, whether of letterpress or illustration, found it difficult or even impossible to dissociate their subject from the 'human element' which enters so persistently into the Beauty of Britain in most of its manifestations. For it must be admitted that it is a beauty that owes much to the friendly care of Englishmen through the centuries; Englishmen have tamed the land from a primeval wilderness to a charming garden, romantic and formal by turns, and have guarded their treasure from the invasion and devastation that have befallen other countries. Rather than replace their buildings they have often preferred to watch them evolve almost organically to their present perfection of age; and in the process, through the use of native materials and perhaps a natural eye for appropriateness and setting, the buildings have grown into and become almost a part of the soil, a legacy from the England of the past to the

vii

England of the present which it is our privilege and duty, and our children's, to preserve.

It is the purpose of this book to set forth some brief account of this man-made Legacy of England, partly in chapters by able and sympathetic contributors, and partly in a collection of photographs which it is hoped will be found representative, though the difficulties of choice have been considerable from the wealth available. It is a book of appreciation, and does not deal, as perhaps it should, with the growing threat to the legacy that seems inherent in modern conditions. There has been no space to discuss the manifold problems of preservation, and the brave fight that different societies and bodies are making against this threat. We can only put forward the hope that anyone who has enjoyed reading these chapters or looking through these illustrations will be impelled in the future to take an active rather than a passive part in the protection of an inheritance, which, however diminished, remains one of the most precious possessions of our race.

CHARLES BRADLEY FORD

October, 1935

2 A CORNER OF OLD NORWICH, WITH A GLIMPSE OF THE
CATHEDRAL

3 THE APPROACH TO LUSTLEIGH, DEVON

Edmund Blunden

~~~~~~

THE
LANDSCAPE

~~~~~~

I DO not know that I can altogether support the French-
man who characterises the Englishman as unable to
steal a goose without moral reflections on the matter.
The pastime of goose-stealing has been too infrequent
here lately for careful observation. But, if that topic is
shelved, there are other instances of what Matthew Arnold
called our divided aims; and the theme of the English
scene brings more than one to my mind. There is
the ardent cricketer, who might be supposed to be
intent only on his swerve, his late cut, or his returns
to the wicket-keeper. Discuss the play with him,
and it appears that what he really came out for was the
Perfect Surroundings—the view of the green, the
church, the woodland, and the highland. I have met
anglers too who defend themselves thus: 'No better
way of being in touch with Nature'—who pursue
anything from a loach to a luce in the real but veiled

passion of discovering river-side landscape and beauties of valley and dell.

With apologies to the aforesaid foreign critic, I believe both these gentlemen entirely. If the anglers in the Maioor Gracht at Ypres were to tell me they were flogging the waters in a spirit of country enchantment, perhaps I might think that I was being used ironically. Even here there are angling competitions. . . .

But to return to the two sportsmen with the vision. Their conversation probably presents an obscurity which embarrasses all who talk or write about their world. It may compress itself into the three guileless-looking words, 'typical English scenery'. Heaven preserve us all from being driven to determine what that really is! It has been settled, in a manner, by the rest of the world. Soon after I arrived in Japan, the old lady who proposed to keep house for me came to me, dictionary in hand and conversation in prospect. She pronounced her *f* in Japanese manner as almost an *b*, and her first remark was, so far as I could catch it, 'Many hogs in England.' Oddly enough, this summer the little hotel-runner in Coblenz said so too—'*Viele Nebel* in England.' Can the League of Nations, in some peaceful interval, attend to this situation?

What can be proposed, in that event, as a simple piece of common knowledge to be substituted for the fog? It is here that the fog really begins. It is to be apprehended that the inhabitants of this kingdom are not at all consonant in their ideas of the typical English scene. There are those whose feelings create it in semblance, let us say, of Epping Forest; others who make of it a perennial Dovedale; others to whom it has been disclosed, a final truth, by John Crome on Mousehold Heath; their rivals whose selection was a little south of that and authorised by Constable. Many a Londoner still escapes from the office to his essential England among the Chilterns, or, it may be, has not yet despaired of it in the Surrey commons. The drunken private of the 'Buffs' in the famous poem saw Kentish hop-gardens beyond his Chinese murderers, and really there is much to be said for them as *the* English scene. At once I seem to hear the protests of my friends now staring in deep moods over the Wuthering Heights expanses. These differences are legion, and often extraordinarily local. I should not like to glorify the Sussex Downs to every Sussex man. Some of that breed have an odd way of seeing England as chiefly the water-meadows by Hardham.

These convictions are usually hinted rather than delimited. But suppose that a Continental inquirer of specially intrepid make were to insist on a solution. I can fancy such a being, who would set aside a number of our highest claims as exceptions; who would refuse to consider the Peak Country, or the Wordsworth Country, or Wild Wales, or the regions west of Saltash Bridge, or the Cheddar Gorge, or the Yorkshire Moors, or all round the Wrekin, or any other colour-poster settings of ours, as characteristic and inimitable. Let this logician be imagined even to have rejected the Cotswolds (and all the blandishments of Mr. H. J. Massingham) on the grounds of a certain eccentricity. Forced thus towards

3

some vaguely central point, I might take temporary shelter behind our old friend, and fine judge of landscape, William Cowper. His England is precisely declared to all comers:

> Here Ouse, slow winding through a level plain
> Of spacious meads with cattle sprinkled o'er,
> Conducts the eye along his sinuous course,
> Delighted. There, fast rooted in his bank,
> Stand, never overlook'd, our fav'rite elms
> That screen the herdsman's solitary hut;
> While far beyond and overthwart the stream
> That as with molten glass inlays the vale,
> The sloping land recedes into the clouds;
> Displaying on its varied side, the grace
> Of hedge-row beauties numberless, square tow'r,
> Tall spire, from which the sound of chearful bells
> Just undulates upon the list'ning ear;
> Groves, heaths, and smoking villages remote.

Or, if Cowper's panorama were still thought to have a tincture of Dutch painting and so gave our prosecutor a fresh objection, safety might be found with a prose gentleman, whose life was gentle but of mixed elements. St. George, and Mr. Pickwick, for merry England. We might go with Mr. Pickwick and Winkle and Snodgrass, to the rescue of the heart-shattered Tupman, all the way to Cobham:

'A delightful walk it was: for it was a pleasant afternoon in June, and their way lay through a deep and shady wood, cooled by the light wind which gently rustled the thick foliage and enlivened by the songs of the birds that perched upon the boughs. The ivy and the moss crept in thick clusters over the old trees, and the soft green turf overspread the ground like a silken mat. They emerged upon an open park, with an ancient hall, displaying the quaint and picturesque architecture of Elizabeth's time. Long vistas of stately oaks and elm trees appeared on every side; large herds of deer were cropping the fresh grass; and occasionally a startled hare scoured along the ground, with the speed of the shadows thrown by the light clouds which sweep across a sunny landscape like a passing breath of summer.

' "If this," said Mr. Pickwick, looking about him; "if this were the place to which all who are troubled with our friend's complaint came, I fancy their old attachment to this world would very soon return."

' "I think so too," said Mr. Winkle." '

All things being duly weighed, Pickwick is probably the Englishman who includes the race (I have seen him even in the battle-field, now as a quartermaster, now as a raider); and correspondingly the kind of countryside through which Dickens makes him move has a strong chance of being the distinctive English scene. That is, as long as any of it is left. It is very alarming that one's thoughts on this subject incline towards past tenses. The mechanisation of our days has certainly disturbed many of those local harmonies which would have rewarded Mr. Pickwick's travels. What one may call the small English scene has been impoverished. A single detail may illustrate this fact: it has actually become necessary to make a census of the surviving windmills in our counties. Who could have thought how rapidly a familiar part of our landscape and our habit would become 'a rare and valuable curiosity'? The great estates, which Richard Jefferies interpreted and without which even Charles Lamb would have been less Elian, have suffered a land change; as poems of greensward, forest tree and pool, they vanish apace. They have been in a manner our oldest and grandest National Gallery—the British School, imitated with delight by many beyond Channel, like the Kurfürst who enriched Munich with its *englischer Garten* —could he but have won the secret of that northern turf!

Yet here, rather than look a short way into the past or the future, I am impelled to view a temporary trouble in relation to a larger period of time. After all, whatever we may individually hold precious as the 'sweet especial English scene', it is likely that its actual existence has been comparatively brief. Were we to be set down in the England of King Canute or even of Charles II, should we find the sort of fascination that moves us, or would those places which have haunted us ever since we first saw them be what they seem now? Perhaps the delicate complexities, the fresh pastorals, the unlonely solitudes which stayed Mr. Pickwick, as Mont Blanc the morning star, would hardly have been there when and if Mr. Pepys passed that way.

In the history of our familiar landscape (I admit with some pain that it is a shadowy abstraction where one would have it sunlit), the age of Samuel Pepys is not least important or emphatic. Endeavouring to recapture the portrait of our land from the much more distant centuries, I confess I am disappointed. A geological 'face of England' through its ancient changes cannot well give that intimate communion which is the inspiration of such tributes as the present work. When the mammoth and tiger and hippopotamus succeeded, in the valley I look upon as I write, to the iguanodon and plesiosaurus, it may be that some of our contours were not utterly dissimilar from these which look eternal now. There were immense dawns, and the evening shadows made gigantic dreams. After the straight-tusked elephant had passed, and I do not know how many thousands of years, I am to conceive that our winding river was not that silver snake whose coilings here and there gleam at the hill-top watcher, but a broad swamp with the pile-dwellings of men flanking its reeds and osiers. Presently there came the temple-builders, who have succeeded in bequeathing a part of this English scene; for high up on the down, grey and solitary, one of their stone shrines is standing yet. May one conjecture that its site was chosen for the clear and spirit-calming scene which it commands there, its strong headstone raised above the plough-land and the sunk lanes? Did its architects work from the feeling that this valley with its deep and steady river, its broad and fruitful lands, was beautiful to contemplate—was a personal presence?

But the conjecture (for which those who know the dawn of history must forgive me) fades into that legend of shaggy forests which clings to the Weald, and which those who travelled into Sussex until the days of George III took with them as part of the adventure. Silva Anderida was once a name yielding meanings almost as strange and troublous as Ethiopia Interior. Long did the Tree with his underwood lord it over this country; great is the catalogue of the ancient forests. Of Silva Anderida, or Andredsweld—to consider this one alone— Drayton in Elizabeth's time sings pensively; notices how it had dwindled into four smaller forests, Ashdown being one; and then how the demands of the ironmasters and consequent rise of speculators had lately ravaged these.

> These Forests as I say, the daughters of the *Weald*
> (That in their heavy breasts had long their griefs con-
>   ceal'd)
> Foreseeing their decay each hour so fast came on,
> Under the axe's stroke, fetch'd many a grievous groan,
> Whenas the anvil's weight, and hammer's dreadful
>   sound,
> Even rent the hollow woods, and shook the queachy
>   ground.

Previously, according to Drayton, the peace of these woods, lately destroyed by timber-wagons, had been broken only by the droves of swine scampering for the mast. He mentions among the trees there the oak, ash, elm, beech, hazel, maple, aspen, wych, holly, and birch.

The thought of such sylvan wildernesses in the early days of English history overcame Mark Twain's satire when he was writing *A Yankee at the Court of King Arthur*, and I would willingly be persuaded that the day-dream he there put into words is a true impression of our

4 THE SEVERN VALE FROM THE COTSWOLD RIDGE AT NYMPSFIELD, GLOUCESTERSHIRE

5 WINTER IN THE PENNINES NEAR APPLETREWICK, YORKSHIRE

country so long before Mr. Pepys, Mr. Pickwick, and ourselves.

'From hill-tops we saw fair green valleys lying spread out below, with streams winding through them, and island-groves of trees here and there, and huge lonely oaks scattered about and casting black blots of shade; and beyond the valleys we saw the ranges of hills, blue with haze, stretching away in billowy perspective to the horizon, with at wide intervals a dim fleck of white or grey on a wave-summit, which we knew was a castle. We crossed broad natural lawns sparkling with dew, and we moved like spirits, the cushioned turf giving out no sound of footfall; we dreamed along through glades in a mist of green light that got its tint from the sun-drenched roof of leaves overhead, and by our feet the clearest and coldest of runlets went frisking and gossiping over its reefs and making a sort of whispering music comfortable to hear; and at times we left the world behind and entered into the solemn great deeps and rich gloom of the forest. . . . And by and by out we would swing again into the glare.'

One must either permit an imaginative writer like Mark Twain to paint that early countryside or do one's best to create a rival fancy of it all; for unfortunately the older literature of England is anything but rich in the treatment of the actual land in which its authors walked and rode. Had there been a firm of Batsford in the reign of the Conqueror, things might have been different. Consulting the chronicler Robert of Gloucester, one gleans only generalisations—not indeed without their savour and colour. England, he says, is a 'well good land', in his opinion the best of the lot, eight hundred miles long from south to north, and four hundred broad in the midland. Full enough of fruit and of trees, of woods and parks ('that joy it is to see'), of fowls and beasts both wild and tame, of salt fish and fresh fish and fair rivers, sweet and cold wells, leas and meadows, silver, gold, tin, lead, steel, iron, brass, good corn, fine wool, fine waterways and harbours. There are many islands around England—the best islands. The chief towns are London, York, Lincoln, Leicester, Colchester, Canterbury, Bristol, Worcester, Chichester, Cambridge, Cirencester, Dorchester, Winchester, and Gloucester. There are three wonders in England: the water of Bath, Stonehenge, and the Hole of the Peak. Fair ways many, and four principal, Fosse Way from Totnes to Caithness the finest, though Watling Street is 'some deal great'. So clean a land and so pure that the handsomest men of the world are born there.

Through such fragmentary things the bright look of that England may be discerned; it is a friendly place. How naturally comes Chaucer forth on his way to Canterbury as it then was! Again, one may collect from his *Tales* a number of occasional touches which afford some consolation for what he did *not* write about his England. Above all, the shadow of a savage scenery does not fall on his brilliant sketch-book. It is singular that one so observant, whose knowledge of the countries over the Channel was not small, and who delighted in the 'form

6 THE MILL-POOL AT FLATFORD ON THE STOUR, SUFFOLK, MADE FAMOUS BY CONSTABLE

7 LOOKING ACROSS THE GRAZING MARSHES TO GLASTONBURY TOR, SOMERSET

of things' in city and upland alike, did not find a day for
some finished study of the English rural scene distinct
from the rest. His readers have gladly looked with him,
at least, into Norfolk, where the Reeve had his dwelling

> full fair, up on an heath:
> With grenë treës shadwed was his place;

or again they never weary of discovering the poor
widow's narrow cottage,

> Beside a grove, standing in a dale,

with the three large sows, three cows, a sheep called Mall,
and in the yard enclosed with sticks and a dry ditch, bold

> Chaunticleer among his wyves all.

Indeed, Chaucer completes that picture. The widow's
smallholding has a cabbage-bed, meadows and hedges
between it and the grove; and when the Fox makes off
with the Cock, the place is filled with suddenly revealed
inhabitants—farm-hands, dogs, ducks, geese frightened
into flight, and bees pouring from their hives. A wider
range is suggested in a few words by the Wife of Bath
beginning her tale, and protesting that the fairies, who
in King Arthur's days danced 'in many a grene mede',
are since scared away by the multitude of

> holy freres
> That serchen every land and every streem,
> As thick as motës in the sunne-beam,
> Blessing hallës, chambres, kitchens, boures.
> Citees, boroughs, castles, hyë toures,
> Thorpës, barnës, shippons, daieries—
> This maketh that there been no faieries.

Here Chaucer shows us the hollow road and the hay-cart coming through it; there the winter scene, the sleet and rain and nothing green and the old year sitting in-doors by his fire; there the dove and swallow on the roof of the barn. By all these tokens we know that his England and our own are not infinitely sundered; and yet there is so much that he might have told us, he whose appointments so often took him into the woodland and chase and farm.

If tradition may be trusted, Chaucer was one of those who played some part in making the beauty of old England. Two centuries and a half after his death (which happened A.D. 1400) Mr. Packer, worthy proprietor of Dennington Park near Newbury, was pointing out three wonderful oaks, planted 'and dedicated' there by Chaucer —the King's, the Queen's, and Chaucer's Oak. Their stature and quality, at any rate, did honour to their planter. They are recorded in the *Sylva* of John Evelyn, a book to which (with some subsidiary writings by the same gentle-man) I shall now turn for notices of the seventeenth cen-tury as an agreeable force in the shaping of our scenery.

There was decided purpose in the air then. Trees, considered as Britain's wealth, armament, and grace, were the passion of many country gentlemen less cele-brated than John Evelyn, Esq., F.R.S. Plantation was a pastime with the royal favour upon it—and here let me introduce, as Evelyn does on an early page,

'old Sir *Harbotle Grimstone*, who (I am told) from a very small Nursery of Acorns, which he sowed in the neglected corners of his ground, did draw forth such numbers of Oaks of competent growth as, being planted about his Fields in even and uniform rows, about one hundred foot from the Hedges, bush'd and well water'd till they had sufficiently fix'd themselves, did wonderfully improve both the beauty and the value of his Demeasnes'.

Let Sir Harbotle be accompanied by 'Mr. Christopher Darell, a Surrey gentlemen of Nudigate', who, though a great ironmaster, had found out means to avoid the reproach aimed by Drayton at his Elizabethan predecessors. For 'he so ordered his Works, that they were a means of preserving even his Woods', by his concern for the whole subject of timber-trees and their 'planting, enclosing and cherishing'. Once, according to Evelyn, the Spanish Armada had received orders, in the event of an incomplete conquest of Britain, at least to leave not a tree standing in the Forest of Dean. The dirge of that forest, subdued not by foreign axes but our own, had been sung by Cowley—but the scientific and country-loving seventeenth century (by Macaulay's leave) had seen better since.

There is a magnificent passage in Evelyn's book on the existing models for country gentlemen to copy, the great houses 'crown'd and incircl'd with stately rows of Limes, Firs, Elms and other ample, shady and venerable Trees', both at a distance from London and within its range.

'Nearer the Metropolis yet are the parks of St. James, Hide-Park, and that sweet Villa (as now built, planted and embellish'd) of Kensington, deserving a particular description; and for all that can be desirable of Magnificence, Hamton-Court, truly Great, in a most beautiful Flat; the Palace, Gardens, Canale, Walks, Groves and Parks; the Sweet and Silent Thames gliding her Silver Streams to the Triumphal Winsorian *Tempe*, raising its Stately Head, and which alone, has in view an Hemisphere, as far as Eyes and Telescopes can distinguish Earth from Heaven: Thus from the Keape, the Terrace, Parks and Forests equalling, nay exceeding any thing *Europe* can boast of.'

The Londoner of to-day will cheerfully applaud the seventeenth century and its genius for a scene 'that is for ever England', on a reading of this mention. 'One needs go no farther to see the effect of this Husbandry, than to St. Jame's Park, where before the Canale, I remember all that pleasant Valley, now yielding most rich Pasturage (with the *Fish*, *Decoy*, and Walks planted with fragrant Lime) was nothing but a noisom unwholsom Bog, and Morass of Moss and Rushes.' But let Evelyn lead us farther afield and show his spirit, to which in him and his contemporaries we still owe so much of our green thought in the green shade.

The subject of hedges, he tells us, ought to interest us. (If we never win a Test match again, we shall still have the world's finest hedges!) He is not merely picturesque about it; he wants his young woods to be safe from 'the venomous bitings and treading of cattel'. Therefore let

8 THE WALL-PATTERNED COTSWOLD UPLANDS

9 THE EXPANSE OF THE BERKSHIRE DOWNS NEAR BLEWBURY

us have some good quickset hedges round them as round other cultivation. The hawthorn makes the best common hedge. Some planters despair, 'not seeing them peep the first year', but Evelyn's instructions will work. He observes that in Herefordshire, every twenty feet along the quickset, they plant a crab-stock—useful for grafting. After three years' growth sprinkle some timber-trees among your hawthorns—oak, beech, ash, maple, fruit, or the like. The art of plashing succeeds to make an 'impregnable' hedge. Some mingle the blackthorn with the white. Evelyn would see the 'preciouser sorts of Thorn and robust Evergreens' made more abundant and brought into the defence—it is their coraline berries as well as their spiny hardihood which he sees coming on among the hips and haws, the cornel and spindle. Nor does he despise a hedgerow of elder, 'every part of the tree being useful', and particularly the medicinal buds and berries.

But he has still to speak of the holly-tree, for use and defence, for sight and ornament. When he does he becomes (to employ an adjective of his own) quite 'rutilant'. Is there, he asks,

'under Heaven a more glorious and refreshing object of the kind, than an impregnable Hedge of about four hundred foot in length, nine foot high, and five in diameter; which I can shew in my now ruin'd Gardens at Say's-Court . . . at any time of the year, glitt'ring with its arm'd and varnish'd Leaves? The taller standards at orderly distances, blushing with their natural Coral; it mocks at the rudest assaults of the Weather, Beasts, or Hedge-Breakers,

Et illum nemo impune lacessit.'

While this bygone worthy worships his 'stately Shrub (as some reckon it)', I for my part fall thinking of the English hedge as being almost as clearly our peculiar inheritance as anything in our country. Here and there in Picardy or in Normandy there will be seen quicksets as beautiful as our own; but ours are ubiquitous. Their white and red may, their bramble-roses, their wild-apple bloom, their honeysuckles, their traveller's joy, have been the spring of the year to most of us more inseparably than any other aspect of the season. By them, from earliest evenings of childhood's freedom to intervals snatched from the dry recurrences of later duty, the footpaths have led, or the tracks of the sheep and cattle to their lairs under the oldest hawthorns. They are the best thing, I think, that the farmer and his labourer in the tattered jerkin have given the wanderer as a rural present. Even in winter an English hedge has, to me, a charm which would be hard to destroy; that thorny criss-cross with the old black nests against the flaming west is what I would ever have to symbolise the departing year. Our greatest dramatist's greatest myth—King Lear, and poor Tom, and the Fool—seems destined to spring out suddenly from these barren shelters, these stubborn, huge-headed oaks amid the entanglement.

Through the sharp hawthorn blows the cold wind.

16

To such agricultural reasoners as Evelyn, and tens of thousands without a pen like his, we owe it largely that this simple treasure, the English hedge, is in our possession. It will last some time yet, though the hedger and ditcher becomes a rarer figure than I can remember him; and when there are no more English hedges, and the expedient of barbed wire has carried the day everywhere,

> Then shall the realm of Albion
> Be brought to great confusion.

Apart from hedges, we are gradually catching up old Mr. Evelyn in a question which hangs over so much of the 'face of England'—Smoke. His campaign for Trees, Trees, and still more Trees was partly one for the public health. He laments that after the Fire of London the magistrates did not

> 'Banish and Proscribe those Hellish Vulcanos, disgorging from the Brew-houses, Sope and Salt-Boilers, Chandlers, Hat-makers, Glass-Houses, Forges, Lime-Kilns, and other Trades, using such quantities of Sea-coals, one of whose Funnels vomits more Smoak than all the Culinary and Chamber-fires of a whole Parish; perniciously infecting the ambient Air, with a black melancholy Canopy, to the detriment of the most Valuable Moveables and Furniture of the Inhabitants, and the whole Country about it.'

This disfigurement, however, was in Evelyn's day mainly confined to London. Its spread has, since he made his complaint, almost prevented us in graver moods from venturing to contemplate the face of England.

But Evelyn offers a philosophy, and sense of proportion, which is as fruitful as his other sylvan precepts. In the hurricane of November 26th, 1703, the oakwoods of England suffered the loss of thousands upon thousands of the bravest trees. Of his own oaks, dear to him as his family, over 2,000 were blown down, 'and this within almost sight of my Dwelling, (now no longer Wotton, Wood-Town) sufficient to mortifie and change my too great Affection and Application to this Work; which, as I contentedly submit to, so I thank God for what are yet left standing: *Nepotibus Umbram*'. In that tranquillity I leave him and his book, but shall think of him as I come in sight of the next cedar in the next rector's garden, or those oaks and beeches that stand 'single in the field' and seen from these hills vary the monochromes of the plain with their blue-shadowy, mantled gianthood.

This old author does not, so far as I can discover, refer to that multitudinous sub-division of the land we inherit, either as characteristic or as curious; much as our silent sense of England includes very prominently the hedgerow along lane-side or between pastures, so therein, in many a tint and many a design,

Like to a map the hills and valleys lie.

It may be that not every observer cares greatly for this inveterate parcelling-out of a land. Certainly it asserts man's failure in pure romanticism, and success in practical farming. Considered as a picture, without further

18

10 A LAKELAND COTTAGE IN BORROWDALE, CUMBERLAND

11 THE ROLLING CHILTERNS NEAR WEST WYCOMBE, BUCKINGHAMSHIRE

argument, it is generally very popular with us. It may answer the kind of orderliness without severity which is apparently a strong element in the English temper. The undulation of our land is almost everywhere sufficient to give us this display of 'wide territory' spread patch-work-quilt fashion towards the horizon, and it is seldom so violent as to make the sight a matter of particular excursion. The delicate colourings which all seasons in this climate beget through field and wood are given us, by this arrangement of farm property, in a gentle and unwearying composition—a vast miniature.

> There see the clover, pea and bean
> Vie in variety of green;
> Fresh pastures speckled o'er with sheep;
> Brown fields their fallow sabbaths keep;
> Plump Ceres golden tresses wear,
> And poppy top-knots deck her hair;
> And silver stream thro' meadows stray,
> And Naiads on the margin play;
> And lesser nymphs on side of hills
> From plaything urns pour down the rills.

So the early eighteenth-century poet rhyme-painted this English mosaic of arable, sward, and woodland.

It is not for me to plunge into the tides of historical, agricultural, and legal theory on the evolution of our farm-lands into such appearances, and wherein originates their main difference from those of France. Folkland, Crownland, Bookland, the three terms under which so much of our modern scene was developed a thousand years since, may be better explored in the natural authori-ties from Maine to Vinogradoff. Whether the ancients enclosed or not, someone did. Someone marked out this Long Acre for Wat and that Little Field for Tib. The lord of the manor is still a name, occasionally an effective one, but once he must have been, to local eyes, as grand a figure as Lear.

> Give me the map there.
> Of all these bounds, even from this line to this,
> With shadowy forests and with champains rich'd,
> With plenteous rivers and wide-skirted meads
> We make thee lady.

But if the manor gave general directions, surely the minor adjustments were derived from the shrewdness of the 'man on the spot'. How much he and his team could best plough in one consideration, which piece would profit most for tillage, for pasture, for shaw, for mill and pond, he, consulting with Nature and the rest of the village, was most competent to settle. The countryman's decision in such affairs is quite likely to remain, once it is taken. The other day I was walking with a map of rather ancient date over the country devasted by the battle of the Somme. Discerning on the map the former existence of an insignificant wagon-track into the wide wheatfields, I ventured to look for it; and there it was once more, as though no fury had ever torn up the whole place in muddy chaos.

Long before Shakespeare's time, then, the polychrome division of England's farm country had been strongly established. The conquerors, and inheritors, and surveyors, and lawyers, and reeves, and wiseacres, and ploughboys had between them all pieced out the soil in

such a way as would later on occasion peace and pleasure
to the age of townspeople escaping from town to the
green hills. As yet, the division was of course not so
elaborate as it was to become, by a long way. But there
were the rival sorts of country: Champion (Shakespeare's
'champain'), or open field; and Several (sometimes
Woodland seems practically of the same force), or enclosed land. And the rivalry was not merely a poetic
idea, but a serious case of contending opinions and
speculations, which by Shakespeare's day had come to a
head in decrees and statutes compelling enclosure, and
the 'insurrection' of cottage farmers resisting it. That
was the time when a farmer (anticipating Mr. Adrian
Bell and Mr. A. G. Street) seized the opportunity and
wrote a best-seller, in rhyme moreover; and in Thomas
Tusser's *Five Hundred Points of Good Husbandry*, which
was revised through numerous editions between 1557
and 1580, we have a propagandist's anthem entitled 'A
Comparison between Champion Country and Severall'.

> The Country inclosed I praise,
>   the tother delighteth not me,
> For nothing the wealth it doth raise,
>   to such as inferiour be
> How both of them partly I know,
>   here somewhat I mind for to shew.

So he begins (no doubt playing with some wheat in
the palm of his hand), and assails Champion roundly.
Unsafe country:

> There swineheard, that keepeth the hog,
>   there neatheard with cur and his horne,

> There shepheard with whistle and dog,
>   be fence to the meadow and corne.
> There horse being tide on a balke
> is ready with theefe for to walke.

Hard work, and little to show for it:

> What laier much better than there,
>   or cheaper (thereon to doe well?)
> What drudgerie more any where,
>   less good thereof where can ye tell?
> What gotten by summer is seene
> in winter is eaten up cleane.

In his mind, Champion is a licensed pirate. Tusser brings on a long catalogue of accusations, such as these:

> The champion robbeth by night,
>   and prowleth and filcheth by day,
> Himselfe and his beast out of sight,
>   both spoileth and maketh away,
> Not onely thy grasse but thy corne,
> both after and yer it be shorne.

Champion means commoners too lazy to work for a living, and lords of the town too indolent to check their knavery. Then

> What foot-paths are made, and how broad,
>   annoyance too much to be borne,
> With horse and with cattell what road
>   is made thorough every man's corne?
> Where champions ruleth the rost,
> there daily disorder is most.

Besides these social disadvantages, there are (Tusser alleges) those of actual production; he contrasts Champion and Several closely:

12 WYRE FOREST FROM KINVER EDGE, WORCESTERSHIRE

13 THE COMBE COUNTRY SOUTH OF EXMOOR, NEAR WINSFORD, SOMERSET

The tone is commended for graine,
   yet bread made of beanes they doe eate:
The tother for one lofe hath twaine,
   of Mastlin, of Rie, or of Wheat.
The champion liveth full bare,
when woodland full merry doe fare.

Tone layeth for turfe and for sedge,
   and hath it with wonderful suit,
When tother in every hedge
   hath plentie of fewell and fruit.
Evils twenty times worser than these,
Enclosure quickly would ease.

These notions of Tusser's were shared by most of
those who had power to act, in and after his time—not
all of them sharing his artless integrity. Onward to the
reign of Victoria the cause of Several Country *versus*
Champion, of enclosure against common, made great
advances, marked by the passing of 4,700 separate Enclosure Acts. When the country could not see anything
ahead but wars and their menace to its food-supply,
patriotism dictated the improvement of our agriculture.
Self-interest crept into the concern, even where one
might least have feared it. A General Enclosure Act at
the end of the eighteenth century was opposed by 'our
long-acred men, who took a false alarm, lest had it been
enacted it would have been the means of reducing the
value of the *old* enclosed lands'. The labouring man had
frequently a simpler and better reason to damn the enclosure party. He merely, in many places, found himself
deprived of immemorial ways and means of life, and
regarded as outside the question which invaded his little

corner. As he looked out at the 'improvements', he felt that his old haunts were undergoing a devastation symbolising the extinction of his traditional, natural existence. Wealth, or, as we should say, Capital, became a demon to his mind; somewhere there was a cruel selfishness of which one tool was Enclosure, and the threatening, the never-weary plough. One labourer had genius to speak out:

Enclosure like a Buonaparte let not a thing remain,
It levelled every bush and tree and levelled every hill . . .

Thus came Enclosure—ruin was its guide,
But freedom's cottage soon was thrust aside,
And workhouse prisons raised upon the site.
Even nature's dwellings far away from men,
The common heath, became the spoiler's prey;
The rabbit had not where to make his den,
And labour's only cow was drove away.

Bitter ghosts must walk where that old battle is now silent and forgotten; and where once-neglected and undrained and half-yielding common-fields have indeed been transformed into mellow cultivation.

The time came when the usefulness of enclosure (to deal with no other aspect) was greatly challenged. Victorian England, whether it looked like it or not, recognised that it lived chiefly by imported provisions. 'It became a matter of little account whether a few more acres of different land were added, or not, to the cultivated area.' Now, from the point of view of the landscape-lover, the situation was pretty good; for, though the long reign of the great gentlemen farmers had largely made our country one great estate, there yet survived a certain element of the primitive and undisciplined. Forest and common, water-meadow and moor, had not all been laid under subjection; their diminished extent, becoming apparent, gave them a new status. A new war began to secure these parts of our softened landscape from the assertions of privilege or assaults of greed. In 1866 the intended expropriation of Berkhamsted Common was countered with organised opposition—there was that dramatic episode, so well chronicled by Lord Eversley, which involved the special train from Euston, its 120 navvies with crowbars, and the demolition by moonlight of two miles of iron enclosure. A pity that the new enterprise had not found its way a few years earlier to Hainault Forest, and to the disadvantage of the contractors' steam-tackle there installed for the sylvan destruction. And the subject is not ended with such retrospective regrets. A new version of enclosure is still —who can forget it?—gnawing away at our landscape inheritance.

In this place the temptation besets me to loiter with the architecture of the past, so much of which has vanished not without blame to ourselves; the sense of what remains has gradually awakened, and has at length secured many a monument that had become Nature's as much as man's. It is nothing new and it is nothing particularly English that old buildings should be doomed when a new age sets itself fresh standards. On reading a history of Ypres, for example, I am almost inclined to think that its enthusiastic citizens themselves abolished the beauties of their city, the best part of a century before

1914, by pulling down almost every ancient wooden house. But if one follows this train of protest far enough back one finds oneself lamenting over the substitution of some great graceful Tudor house for a blunt, gaunt demi-castle; and I shall accordingly resume the main theme of landscape consciousness, in which the preservation of ancient monuments finds its place.

Almost as long as the Englishman has been pursuing the improvement of his land through bush and briar, he has been discovering the beauty of that land. Drayton, whose resentment against the forest-felling ironmasters has been seen, is probably the earliest writer to go into the matter—in that enormous poem *Polyolbion* he is topographer first of all, antiquary next, yet landscapist by turns. Something of the professional writer, narrowly skilful and fluent, makes the passage through the thirty books of *Polyolbion* unexciting in the long run; but he sometimes displays a particularity not too common in Elizabethan descriptions of the land. He is happiest in the Forests, finding

> Fine, sharp, but easy hills, which reverently are crown'd
> With aged antique rocks, to which the goats and sheep
> (To him that stands remote) do softly seem to creep
> To gnaw the little shrubs, on their steep sides that grow;
> Upon whose other part, on some descending brow,
> Huge stones are hanging out, as though they down
>   would drop,
> Where under-growing oaks on their old shoulders prop
> The others' hoary heads.

When we pass into the seventeenth century and hear what Milton has to say in *L'Allegro* and *Il Penseroso*, or

26

14 SUNSET AND SNOW ON REIGATE HEATH, SURREY

15 GRANITE QUARRIES AND OLD MINE WORKINGS ON THE CORNISH MOORS

Walton in his *Compleat Angler*, we recognise a subtler spirit of delight in the English landscape—not a computation of the places one ought to see and their special exhibits but an impression of many places, many moments, blending into a pastoral dream. Then, too, we begin to see the townsman to whom the country is a passion and a thing apart; then comes Milton's significant picture of the man who, 'long in populous city pent', at length has the luck to be out of it and glorying in the ordinary signs and incidents of the countryman's world, to him extraordinary and exquisite. Neither Milton nor Walton, any more than Chaucer, seems curious about the further possibilities of England; mountains and lakes and moors, or the coasts and estuaries, are not perceptibly within their spheres of interest.

That exemplary member of Parliament in Milton's time, Andrew Marvell, opening the poem on the Hill at Bilborow, rebukes mountains in his whimsical fashion,

> Which do, with your hook-shouldered height,
> The earth deform, and heaven fright,
> For whose excrescence ill design'd
> Nature must a new centre find.

Mountains being disqualified, he proves himself a master of the English scene in park-land and pasture—the poet laureate of our sun-burnt hayfields, and our old patriarchal trees by noble houses. Soon afterwards we discover in the Duchess of Newcastle's writings, and the Countess of Winchilsea's, delightful evidences that the familiar, gentle, hamlet landscape was not passed by as unbeautiful in the growing enthusiasm for splendid, spacious, and formal gardens. At the close of the seventeenth century we have the naturalist John Ray looking away alike from village walls and greens, and avenues, vistas, and lawns, to mountains.

'The present Earth looks like a Heap of Rubbish and Ruins. There appear not the least Footsteps of any Art or Counsel, either in the Figure and Shape, or Order and Disposition of Mountains and Rocks.' In such amusing terms did Ray put the case which he wished to refute. First, he maintained, a country with variety of hills and valleys and inequalities was 'far more grateful to behold' than a level; and he instanced on one hand the flat expanse round Ely and on the other the Downs of Sussex and their 'spacious and ravishing Prospect'. Next he supported the Creator's weakness for mountains by pointing out their benefits as 'convenient Places for Habitation', as shelters from winds and traps for sunbeams; and then there must be reckoned the sorts of animals which the mountains enabled to live, and again the plants, the vegetables, and the simples; as also metals and minerals; and even the pasture-lands which supported 'multitudes of kine and many dairy-houses' even in the high Alps. For Ray, in his 'simpling voyages' had been in the Alps, and had liked it. I hope somewhere in the Wordsworth Country, not to mention the South Downs, to find one day a little memorial stone to John Ray.

In the days of Queen Anne the country spirit seems to have been slightly discountenanced by the wits, like Pope, whose Works include an entertaining copy of verses proving to a young beauty what an awful life she would have of it if she were misled out of town. Pope himself saw plenty of England with a curious pleasure—but his world was metropolitan. He witnessed the surprising release of feeling towards the English scene which the publication of James Thomson's *Seasons* in the seventeen-twenties and thirties brought about. Written in blank verse, when people read verse without patting themselves on the back for their martyrdom and kindness to animals, the *Seasons* was a sort of gospel of Beautiful Britain. In that book, a poet who might have been a painter, and who had a wide knowledge of paintings, offered a religion of which the temple was the visible diurnal scene, reflected in his art with a fullness never expressed in our literature before. The multitude, ready for this sun-shaft, followed Thomson's genius with joy. Nor was he quite alone in his philosophy of the benevolent beauty, the inspiring grandeur, waiting for man's friendship in pine-forest and in tangled lane. He was even anticipated by a Welshman named Dyer, who was in fact painter as well as poet, and who in the lyrical lines called 'Grongar Hill' made his words do what he did less famously in his water-colours.

Thenceforward the eighteenth century achieved its sense of landscape and nature with steady subtilisation. Its pilgrims (apart from their migrations into foreign parts) began even to prefer the romantic to the rural scene. Defoe had not so long before scribbled some peevish objections to the Northern Heights of London, as consisting of nothing but ups and downs; but the new generation not only took over Hampstead as a picturesque place of residence but struck out for heights considerably further north. The lakes of Ullswater, Keswick, and Windermere, 'with such beautiful colourings of rocks, wood, and water, backed with so tremendous a disposition of mountains', had called forth eloquent solemnities before Wordsworth came. It was before his time that somebody exclaimed, at a first view of Derwentwater, 'Here is beauty indeed—beauty lying in the lap of horror!' Some, like Dr. Johnson, even went through Scotland in their excitement. Many kept journals or dispatched long letters, like Thomas Gray, in the desire of sharing their mountains and precipices and cascades and glens with those left behind among the haymakers or the hackney coaches.

One of the most voracious appetites for English landscape ever bestowed on mankind was that which the Reverend William Gilpin, A.M., Vicar of Boldre in New Forest, attempted to satisfy in a series of tours. As he was an amateur artist with an exquisite sense of effect, he was able to illustrate the numerous resulting works of description—often reprinted in the last years of the eighteenth century—with aquatints that still allure the fancy. He worked out, what has not survived so well as the aquatints, a critical system of Picturesque Beauty, which delivered him up duly to the comic author who metred out the *Tours of Doctor Syntax*. Almost his earliest excursion, in the summer of 1770, was to the River Wye, along which the poet Gray, almost in the last year of his life, was also finding 'no bad harvest' of beautiful aspects. With what rapture, beyond any 'coherent observations' at the time, did Gilpin on his

16 THE LAKE DISTRICT: LOOKING ACROSS DERWENTWATER TO SKIDDAW, CUMBERLAND

way view the Vale of Severn! Even grander exaltations
awaited him when storm and sun fought out their battle
above him in the mountains. He is disappointing, it is
true, on his homeward route, when he complains that
'Marlborough down is one of those vast dreary scenes
which our ancestors, in the dignity of a state of nature,
chose as a repository of their dead'.

But as this is not the occasion for detailed notes on
Gilpin's tours, I hasten to allude to a chapter of his which
probably transmits much of the spirit of his contemporaries in regarding landscape and travel. It introduces his
Northern Tour, and amounts to a manifesto in favour
of England the beautiful. First sketching the dominant
features of the country—the coasts, the mountains, 'the
great central *patria* of chalk'—he declares that 'this country
exceeds most countries in the *variety* of its picturesque
beauties. I should not wish to speak merely as an Englishman: the suffrages of many travellers and foreigners
of taste, I doubt not, might be adduced.' Allowing
certain notches of superiority to Switzerland, Germany,
and Italy, he still supposes that 'on the *whole*, England
transcends them all. It exhibits perhaps more variety . . .
than is anywhere to be seen in so small a compass.'
Gilpin next attributes to it 'some beauties which are
peculiar to itself'. The mingling of wood and cultivation
is one—not found, he thinks, in France, in Italy, in Spain.
It is the English hedgerow which he has in mind. Seen
too near, he condemns the 'divisions of property' as
formal and unpleasing; 'but when all these regular forms
are softened by distance—when hedgerow trees begin to

unite, and lengthen into streaks along the horizon', then he blesses the English farm-land scene. He thinks the oak too has much to do with the charm—'the noblest ornament of a foreground', and in a distance glorious in shapes and colours. Still gazing, he commends as especially ours the park scene, lawn, wood, and water, 'meditated wild'—he too with the rest of us believes our verdant lawn incomparable for freshness and velvet. Haziness, mist, fog—that sleepy fraternity—receive his blessing, too, as imparting their harmony and mystery to the English scene; and finally he observes that we have the right sort of ruins, castles (others have castles), and abbeys ('where popery prevails, the abbey is still entire and inhabited; and of course less adapted to landscape'). I imagine, somewhere among Gilpin's papers, there was an Ode to Henry VIII, Relative to Picturesque Beauty.

These disorderly scraps of landscape history need not much continuation. Wordsworth and Coleridge need only to be named; the taste for the romantic region had grown towards maturity. The painters of England had grown confident and capable. From the genius and wisdom of some of them it is reasonable to trace a restoration of simple feeling about English landscape. The wonder and majesty of Wordsworth's high argument, 'from Glaramara's inmost caves', might have led the already mountain-trained sensibility too strongly. If that were so, then timely came the golden hours which De Wint's brush eternised by the usual English river taking his easy way through undramatic lowlands towards peeping spires. The Norwich School, modestly superintended by John

Crome, was worth attention. After all, there might be some Wordsworthian voices in the Pyrenees, but the Poringland Oak would be hard to transplant. Next Constable exploded the theory, stubbornly held in some quarters, that colour was un-English; and presently (for my catalogue grows heavy) Birket Foster filled the Christmas books of the Victorians with quiet reminders of the grace they should look for ten or twenty miles from town.

What landscape shall we leave to posterity? Fast as the look of England has changed hitherto, it seems to alter faster now. Forecast is of small value. The unplanned results of activity are often the most lasting; it may be so in landscape. The farmers of two centuries ago came to these hill-sides below my window for lime. Their excavations were extended into huge quarries, which yielded the commercial article, and were abandoned. They might have been disfigurements; but the hand of Nature, the magic of sunlight, 'the unimaginable touch of Time' and quite a few blackberry brambles have seized upon them and something like Picturesque Beauty has ripened.

Adrian Bell

~~~~~~

THE
FARM

~~~~~~

Little Boy Blue, come blow up your horn,
The sheep's in the meadow, the cow's in the corn.

THIS is a literal picture of old English farming: the
animals, pastured on the common, were left in the
care of the village herdsman while their owners were
away cultivating the strips they held in the arable fields
of the village. If the minder of the cattle dozed, then
they strayed into the corn or the meadows reserved for
the working stock, for all was open country, and seldom
a hedge or fence prevented them.

As a child, one's chanting of the nursery rhyme con-
jured a vague picture of the scene, and a sense of the
crisis being even more indefinitely resolved by the blowing of the horn. But of course the horn was a summons
that the stock had been trained to obey; at its sound they
gathered to the herdsman, and were then driven back to

18　A WAYSIDE DRINK AT SAUNTON, NORTH DEVON

10. A FARM GROUP AT BRILL, BUCKINGHAMSHIRE

the village, where the herd split up, every man's beasts going into their separate lodgings. The English village *was* the English farm. The land was divided into arable and pasture and was farmed communally: the rest was 'waste'—heaths, woodlands, roadsides, etc.—over which the cottagers had the right to pasture their beasts, cut fuel and tree-loppings for winter fodder. It is not the object of this article to give a history of farming, but only to indicate the growth and changes that lie behind the word 'farm' as understood to-day.

Even in 1935 the agricultural labourer does not speak of cultivating his garden but of 'farming' it. He is, or has been till recently, the one constant factor in our social structure; his family tree the true continuity. It is quite possible, as village records show, for successive genera-tions of a single family to have farmed on the open-field farm, to have laboured landless after the enclosures, and to-day to be tending a tractor or mechanical milker on the same spot.

There are two ways of looking at the farm and its processes, cultural and economic. Originally there was no such distinction; the people grew what they grew for their own needs, and in the process were closely identified with the changing seasons. They lived entirely in the yearly cycle; and a purpose, tradition, and rhythm were established among them that were a true reflection of their environment.

'In those parishes which afford a most complete example of a social hierarchy and where agrarian change had not deprived the peasantry of rights on the soil, the life of a labourer might be itself more instructive and intelligible than that of his counterpart, the urban artisan. His work at home and in the field afforded a more varied range of experience, in which the relation of means to ends was easily grasped. He saw the nature and meaning of his industry, often the whole processes and their connection with social and domestic needs. . . . His wife span for domestic uses and trained her children in the household arts. . . . And not only was the supply of daily needs a labour which conveyed its own lesson, inspired interests and exercised habits of organisation and self-discipline; but the intimate relations subsisting between the various functions of a village group, the natural correspondence between the parts of a fabric which was the result of age-long growth, rendered its life in some measure an intelligible whole. The appearance of a self-acting community, developing its own discipline, culture, and outlook on the world, was preserved in the administration of open-field husbandry, and more generally in the round of common amusements and the whole body of rustic traditions and beliefs.'[1]

As a sidelight on what our agriculture grew into from such beginnings, there are Cobbett's reflections on riding through the fertile Avon Valley:

'The stack-yards down this valley are beautiful to behold. They contain from five to fifteen banging

[1] A. E. Dobbs: *Education and Social Movements* 1700–1850.

wheat ricks, besides barley ricks and hay ricks, and also besides the contents of the barns. . . . A very fine sight this was, and it could not meet the eye without making one look round (and in vain) to see the people who were to eat all this food and without making one reflect on the horrible, the unnatural, the base and infamous state in which we must be, when projects are on foot, and are openly avowed, for transporting those who raise this food, because they want to eat enough of it to keep them alive. . . .

'A little while before I came to this farm-yard I saw a sheep-fold which, I thought, contained an acre of ground, and had in it about four thousand sheep and lambs. . . . At one farm . . . I counted more than three hundred hogs in one stubble.

'I should suppose that every labouring man in this valley raises as much food as would suffice for fifty or a hundred persons, fed like himself.'

Farming had become a business, and the principle of profit superseded the principle of subsistence—for all except the labourer, the descendant of that same cottager or open-field farmer, who had now no arable strip, no grazing right, no cow. But instead of these things, a wage (at the time of Cobbett's ride, of nine shillings a week). He was still at the subsistence level, but no longer because winter followed summer, no longer organically, but economically, by the working of a system. He was literally cut off with a shilling.

Now we all in our childhood have an impression of

the country that preceded the farming country we know to-day. In nursery-rhymes, in fairy-tales, in such books as the *Pilgrim's Progress*, the scene is the England of open-field farming; the England of wolf-inhabited forests and wastes where squatters cleared a little ground and built themselves huts from the materials to hand—in some places stone, in others dried clay and beams and reeds. Between village and village there was little communication. The manor was the centre of government.

To us to-day it is a sort of dream-country; the unknown lurked over every hill, in every wood. Swamps, heaths, forests divided one cultivated region from another. The strongly physical basis of Bunyan's allegory is significant—he himself being an itinerant: the Slough of Despond, the feudal Doubting Castle; the man with the muck-rake, the Delectable Mountains, Deadman's Lane, where murders were done, and the many roughnesses and uncertainties of the way. I think that this indefinite yet powerful and, if you will, childish impression of the country of fable is not without its relation to fact, in which things by their forms and hues were significant of witchery or god-head, fear or love, death or life. The very opposite in intensity of—shall we say?—the sightseers' point of view. I am not concerned with superstition as such, but with the extent that the whole being of man was continuously roused and aware. Wisdom in that pre-scientific age was an intuition of the wholeness of Nature by the observed interaction of many diverse elements, and a sort of prescience thus evoked; the remains of which may still be found in the

20 CROSSWAYS FARM NEAR ABINGER, SURREY, MADE FAMOUS BY MEREDITH

21 A COTSWOLD FARMYARD AT WINSON IN THE COLN VALLEY

22 SHEEP IN A NORFOLK LANE

unlettered countryman's 'knowledge'; his power of fore-casting the weather by signs. Yet in speaking of 'Nature', of 'knowledge', we cannot help speaking as of something outside ourselves or attached to ourselves, whereas the characteristic of these folk was and is their complete identification with their environment. Even in the matter of weather-signs, or the appraisement of animals, it has been suggested that the countryman's power is even less conscious than appears; he *knows*, he has a *feeling* as to this or that, and he puts it on to variable signs and 'points', which are not, as he thinks, the actual source of his insight.

However that may be, we have only to look at the shapes of traditional farm implements to see how men's ideas followed Nature, line for line. To cut the grass man evolved a blade like a blade of grass; and he went into the wood and cut a pole growing with a compen-sated curve for handle; because he found that that im-plement harmonised best with the balance and rhythm of his body for the purpose. From rude beginnings the scythe has been perfected to a scientific instrument, but always following, as it were, this curve of Nature, till the setting of a scythe to the satisfaction of the expert became a problem geometrically related to stance and arm's length; measured, of course, by eye. Thus, to the curve of natural symmetry that every leaf has, another, invisible, was added—the curve of economy and rhythm in pro-cess. So the plough, starting as a pointed stick, became invested with coulter, share, 'ground', and wrest; and finally, in the last stages of horse cultivation, became an instrument of nice adjustment and lightness of balance. Here again, the beauty of the 'warp' of a plough wrest, shining from friction with the earth, is movement statically expressed; the whole process of the turning of a furrow is implicit there. The pitchfork started as a branched stick, the harrow as a bush, the roller as a log. The cart and wagon, from a clumsy structure on solid wheels, evolved into a grace of combined lightness and strength, became differentiated for use on a variety of soils and for many purposes, from the dung-cart that must stand the flinging of the whole weight first on one wheel and then on the other as it traverses ground that yesterday was slush and to-day is frozen clods, to the farmer's fast gig with wheels lost in light in motion. To different districts their different lines and proportions: deep or narrow bodies—'bucks'—wide or narrow wheels. I know of a wagon, and a new one at that, built of elm, oak, and ash, with *walnut* fittings. What was it gave to the old road wagons, especially when newly painted and 'lined out', a richness almost galleon-like? Not primarily the desire to decorate, but the need to shave away every particle of surplus weight. Thus straight edges became chamfered, and projections were finely tapered. The problem of locking the front wheels is responsible for much of the shape of a wagon. The wheels could not be made smaller on account of the mud; or the floor raised on account of the height of a man and the balance of a load—hence curved-in sides, lifted fronts.

Before the recent break in continuity, agricultural craftsmanship was a thing of evolution and inheritance, of which every branch was interwoven with the whole. The wheelwright used timber which his father had laid down for him, and his education was through his hands. There are at this moment three tumbrils standing in a cart-shed; one was made by a local wheelwright, the son of a wheelwright, the other two came from a factory. Leaving out of account the difference in the quality of the materials, the factory-made carts cause the men twice as much trouble in tipping and loading and are much heavier in draught than the locally made one. The latter can be tipped, when loaded, by one man with ease, the others hardly by the whole gang. They hinder work, the other helps. Thus the trades dependent on agriculture grew out of it: before being a wheelwright the man was a farmer, potentially at any rate, and a local one at that.

The country that is before our eyes to-day is so completely 'England' that it is difficult to visualise it in any other form. Yet even now there are places and moments in which the spirit of an earlier England seems to dwell. One comes on them by chance. For what they are worth I will tell of two such occasions I remember. One was in the autumn; a dark day on which winter seemed nearer than the slightly tinted woods foretold. The ruined abbey was carpeted with short grass thoughout, the more vividly green for the protection or the shadow of the walls; all this looking strangely young and spruce beside the antiquity of the stone, which seemed to be returning to its wild unwrought state less by erosion than by something implicit in its nature, when the power and purpose for which it was articulated were withdrawn. Through the shattered delicacy of the great window I saw a sow and her litter nuzzling under oak-trees. A man dug on a small plot; smoke drifted. For the rest, woods hung upon the steep sides of the valley as they had always done. It was a medieval picture; in that moment time lapsed back a thousand years. The *Te Deum* of the window; the primitive monosyllable of the cottar's hut; the one contained within the other in strange, complete harmony. I reflected then how the monks in their day had kept alive the arts of agriculture. Here they had studied the ancient writers, Cato, Virgil, Varro; they had undertaken drainage, reclamation; built roads and bridges. The monasteries were the centres of culture—religious, intellectual and domestic. It was a culture in no way departmentalised, but single to the extent that the dweller in the primitive hut could 'understand' the beauty of the abbey and feel its power; and the ecclesiastic, looking out of his window, knew what that man was about, his times and seasons, the uses of his tools. He was not just a man digging or ploughing. One could not but feel the loss of such a synthesis, especially at that time and in that weather; the place reverting to its own inaccessible life after the summer's trippers had departed, the sky closing down upon that valley, cold and grey and aged-seeming as the balanced walls, making it a place of stillness and water-echoes.

On another occasion, in brusque spring weather, I was passing through the Fens, and came upon an expanse of common pasture, several acres in extent. Beside it stood

23 SHEEP ON A FARM IN SUFFOLK

24 SHEEP GRAZING AT WITHERMARSH GREEN ON THE STOUR, SUFFOLK

25 HARVEST-TIME ON SHALDON HILL, SOUTH DEVON

small cottages in the dull grey brick of the district, while geese, poultry, horses and cattle roamed the green. There was washing hanging out, and here and there a pile of faggots, bee-hives, a segment of a stack of hay, and a rough shed or two of boards and brushwood. In one corner was a group of caravans, where wild-haired children played, while their parents were engaged in grooming and preparing a troupe of brisk brown-and-white pie-bald ponies. An oldish man stood at a little distance leaning on a staff observing this, while the animals that grazed on the common advanced ever nearer to the edge of the corn behind his back. For the common ended and small strips and plots of corn-land began, without any barrier between them; and on every plot and strip a man was working, and sometimes a man and a woman; some were hoeing, some singling beet plants, some weeding with their hands. The intentness and anxiety of their labour was remarkable only to anyone unacquainted with the Fens; the hoers were bent almost double, holding their tools far down the handles; while the singlers crawled along the ground on their hands and knees. The women wore great starched sun-bonnets; their faces peered out from tunnels of shade. One old woman I met on the road, her hoe over her shoulder, after six in the evening. Her face impressed me, though there was nothing outstanding about it that I could see; in fact there was something so universal about it; so devoid was it of the lines and expression that personal experience engrave upon the flesh, that it seemed to shine, smooth like a washed-up stone. She was dazed, perhaps, with the long day's work in the hedgeless fields, yet she seemed entirely composed; it was rather as though the great distances of earth and sky, the eventfulness of the latter weighing upon the monotony of the former, had so continually met in her as to crowd out anything that could privately 'matter'; till she was happiness without a smile, incurious alertness, activity without desire. The very opposite of the keen fatiguing cares in house-wives' eyes. She was a focus, rather, a reflection of the evening light; aware of what was immediate—the road, my passing, the sky, and the brisk wind from the sea. Looking at her I felt the limits of personality recede indefinitely. She was, in fact, the Fens.

If this impression of the wide common, with its fringe of cottages, and the corn-land beyond in hedgeless plots, is a picture, though illusory, of an earlier England, there is another part of this country that well represents the kind of waste that lay between cultivation and cultivation. I mean Wicken Fen. It is one of the few pieces of original undrained fen, abounding in rare moths and butter-flies, though they themselves are in part due to a by-product of agriculture—the traditional cutting of the reeds by the inhabitants for thatching. These reeds were once an important source of income to the people—so much so that the fen used to be portioned off among them for that purpose. But with modern building the demand has almost ceased. Yet this cutting allowed the wild plants to thrive on which these insects fed, so where-as once the object of legislation was to bring more land into cultivation, here wildness, under the National Trust, is carefully preserved, and the reed-cutting undertaken for the sake of the wild life. To see this piece of primitive England is to realise the concealment afforded to fugitives and outlaws years ago. To-day, in the reclaimed fen-lands, a man can be seen three miles off—in Wicken Fen hardly three yards. It is not just the wildness, but the feeling of it—the feeling of an unknown world.

Now this old system of farming, communal within the protective feudal framework, suited those social conditions in which money did not predominate. It would not be too much to say that the principal unit of coinage was the day's work of an able-bodied man and eight oxen —an acre of ploughing. Thus the tenant paid his rent to his lord. But with the birth of industrialism something more than the manorial system broke up: the elaborate economy—dovecots, fish-ponds, spinning-wheel, etc.—whereby a village community was self-supporting, broke up too. A town population and a country population became reciprocal, and the principle of money-profit was introduced. Slowly at first, and latterly more generally, the open-field strips began to be laid together and enclosed. More and more food must be produced, to make a profit and pay for the manu-facturers' profit and feed a growing population. Yester-day's luxuries became the necessities of to-day; and so life became less of a struggle with Nature and more of a struggle between man and man.

Improved farming could not have come about under the old system. Innovations are made by the curious few, never by a three-fourths majority of a community.

In Tudor times many writers championed open-field farming; in the eighteenth century nearly all were for enclosures. The difference in outlook is significant—significant also that the culture of the later age could see little beauty in wild nature. The reversion to pasture for sheep had ceased, and enclosure now meant increased corn-production. The Napoleonic war made this increase essential. The farm must be turned into a food-factory at all costs. And it was done. By the end of the war, modern rural England was in existence.

That increased production—the criterion of farming *as a business*—was only to be achieved through enclosed farms, all were agreed (Cobbett, perhaps, excepted). As to the moral consequences of turning the peasant off his common, arguments were not lacking when the need was proved. The tithe-owners, now that enclosure meant corn, turned over to the side of enclosure. It was alleged that the ownership of a cow and common rights made the peasant idle and shiftless. He had too much time to 'stand and stare'; and was not ambitious enough to increase his material well-being by working hard all day. His children were brought up to sloth and nonchalance; the commons were the devil's playground. 'The men seem to be very lazy'; 'the people poor, ignorant, and slothful'; 'many brawling contentions'; 'the resort of the most idle and profligate of men.' Such was the gist of many reports, scientifically undertaken; few voices were raised on the other side. In the light of this it is interesting to read Cecil Sharp's introduction to *English Folk Songs of the Southern Appalachians*. He found a people living isolated from the rest of the world, whose ancestors had emigrated from England in the eighteenth century. They talked English, not American, and 'from the number of expressions they use which have long been obsolete elsewhere, and the old-fashioned way in which they pronounce many of their words, it is clear that they are talking the language of a past day'.

He found them living in extreme simplicity with practically no available markets and very little money. Each family grew just what it required to live on; no more. In fact 'many set the standard of bodily and material comfort perilously low, in order, presumably, that they may have the more leisure and so extract the maximum enjoyment out of life'. He found 'people naturally dignified and cultured, though illiterate. Although uneducated in the sense in which that term is usually understood, they possess that elemental wisdom, abundant knowledge, and intuitive understanding which only those who live in constant touch with Nature and face to face with reality seem able to acquire. . . . The Mountaineer bears no trace of that obsequiousness of manner which, since the Enclosure Acts, has unhappily robbed his British prototype of his economic independence and made of him a hired labourer.' He visited the Appalachians in order to collect the old songs and ballads which were still sung there. In England he could only discover these among the aged, but with these people the young sang them as spontaneously as the old.

Here was a community interested more in leisure than increased production, and he bears witness to the 'many graces of life that were theirs'. It is a fascinating picture of what people whom an eighteenth-century observer would have labelled 'poor, ignorant, and slothful' could make of life.

Even Arthur Young, one of the warmest advocates of enclosure, lived to regret some of its effects, and tried to call a halt to the divorcing of the peasant from the land. But too late.

Yet in the England of the middle of last century, the England of the large farm and capitalist yeoman, we have here and there a picture of a social organism, a kind of latter-day feudalism, which is not without its merits. In the *Life of George Crabbe* by his son there is an account of the establishment of a typical yeoman, that of his uncle, Mr. Tovell of Parham in Suffolk. The house had a spacious hall paved with black and white marble, draw-ing-room and dining-room, yet one side overlooked a farm-yard, and except on state occasions the family lived in the old-fashioned kitchen.

'My great uncle occupied an arm-chair, or, in attacks of gout, a couch on one side of a large open chimney. Mrs. Tovell sat at a small table, on which, in the evening, stood one small candle in an iron candle-stick, plying her needle by the feeble glimmer, sur-rounded by her maids, all busy at the same employ-ment; but in winter a noble block of wood, sometimes the whole circumference of a pollard, threw its com-fortable warmth and cheerful blaze over the apart-ment. . . .

'The family dined in this wise: the heads seated in the kitchen at an old table; the farm-men standing in an adjoining scullery, door open; the female servants at a side table called a *bouter*; with the principals at the table, perchance some travelling rat-catcher or tinker, or farrier, or an occasional gardener in his shirtsleeves, his face probably streaming with perspiration. . . .'

In another contemporary picture of life on a big farm we find the farmer sitting on one side of his kitchen hearth, the men on the other, discussing with one another the work of the morrow.

Already farming had become to an extent departmentalised. The Midlands had gone down to grass; hops were concentrated in Kent, fruit in the West; Eastern England was almost entirely arable. Coke of Norfolk had turned rabbit-warrens into corn-land by green crops, stock, and manuring; Jethro Tull had invented the drill, whereby corn was sown in straight lines instead of broadcast; with its corollary, the horse-hoe. Bakewell had started the scientific breeding of horses and cattle. In most districts a plough drawn by two horses and driven by one man had been an unheard-of economy —six horses and three men in some places being employed upon the old cumbersome machine.

Now, under the rule of the capitalist farmer, a new organism replaced the old community of small open-field farmers, socially and economically self-contained, if no longer self-supporting. The four-course shift became the unit of cultivation, and stock were made much more scientifically reciprocal with the land. The labourer had been taken from his commons and welded into this new organisation as a skilled hand. He developed his prowess upon certain lines—some became cowmen, others plough-men, stock-feeders, stackers, thatchers, carpenters, gar-deners; till in course of time there were ploughmen that could not milk and cowmen that could not plough. Yet the standard of specialised skill became a very high one. And this kind of farm drew into its orbit innumerable minor tradesmen, as in the *Life of George Crabbe* we see a rat-catcher, farrier, or gardener at the farmer's table. The peasant had lost his independence, but he was not yet cut off socially from his superiors. Perhaps the economic results of enclosures mattered ultimately less to him than the social one. The farm kitchen had at first a resem-blance to the feudal hall; employer and employed might disagree, but they were fundamentally as man to man, and understood each other. But as industrialism progressed the farmer and his wife approximated more to the 'polite' classes; they withdrew into their parlours, apart from farm-hands and maids, till it would have become an em-barrassment for both employer and employed to sit down at the same table. Less and less farm-servants lived in; till finally the modern condition is reached. There stands the large, rambling old farm-house, full of unused rooms. At one end of it sit the master and mistress in what is called a 'breakfast-room'; at the other end a solitary young maid in cap and apron in the kitchen, flanked by an empty cheese-room and dairy. This was perhaps the greatest blight that fell upon agriculture in its social

26 KENTISH OAST-HOUSES AND CHERRY ORCHARDS NEAR PADDOCK WOOD

aspects. Only the other day an old woman showed me a long steel fork like a minature hay-fork with which, she said, they used to get the meat and dumplings out of the copper in which the harvest dinners were cooked on the farm where she had started work as a dairymaid. While a modern, highly specialised farmer said, 'If only one could get rid of these farm hands, and get, say, some unemployed miners from Wales, or cotton-spinners, or iron-workers—because then you could teach them what to do in the way you want it done; but with these people whose families have lived here since the beginning of time, why, do you think I can get the horse-keeper to feed half a dozen bullocks while he is doing his horses, or the cowman at a pinch to do a day's ploughing? It's as bad as the caste system in India!'

But traditional usage cannot be discarded like an old garment by those who have been for generations bent to its service. After enclosures the dispute was: large or small farms. The tendency has been for the size of the farm to increase. There are many farm-cottages dotted about the country to-day, often down lanes inaccessible to modern traffic, which upon closer inspection prove to have once been farm-houses themselves. Here and there an ancient barn and a yard may be seen, with perhaps a gnarled apple-tree or two as the only remaining sign that a house once stood there also. An old man of nearly a hundred who had lived in one district all his life was able to give quite a different topography of the place from that now seen. Fields had been thrown together, hedges and ditches obliterated; and quite a number of other things that once went hand in hand with local agriculture had disappeared. 'Here,' he said, pointing to a dip in a field, 'there used to be a brick-kiln; and in the dairy and kitchen of yonder farm the bricks that used to be baked here cover the floor. Anyone used to be able to see five mills from hereabouts, but now you can't only see one, and that's got two sails broke off.'

The large farm absorbed these smaller occupations, usually because the few acres that went with a mill or with one of the large cottages contained some warm paddocks useful for calved heifers or weanlings; or because they drove wedge-like into the larger farmer's boundary and offered a vantage-ground for poachers of his game. He had the money and was prepared to pay a higher price than the would-be small occupier could afford.

While agriculture throve even moderately the large farm often represented a considerable degree of security for all within its framework. The master's command of capital and credit was flexible enough to take the strain of variable prices and seasons and maintain a steady level of employment to the workers. The workers' sons grew up to take the places of their fathers, their daughters were received as kitchen- or dairymaids. This kind of farm of mixed stock-breeding and arable cultivation on the four-course shift survived until recently. With improvements in reaping and threshing machinery it became a model of clean and efficient husbandry. In it, intensive production and high individual skill in the labourer seem to have met at their peak. I see it as that balance between hand-labour and machinery allied and not opposed, which is the professed ideal of the future, actually achieved. Artificial fertilisers were used freely, but sheep and farm-yard manure from cake-fed cattle were recognised as the indispensable basis of fertility. The reaper-and-binder and the elevator lightened the labour but detracted little from the skill of harvest. The arts of pitching, loading, stacking, and thatching were as essential as ever. If corn was no longer carried to the merchant's always by by road, the wagons still went to and fro between the farm and the railway station.

Yet even since the war I have known wagons make the whole journey to the town where the corn was sold, a distance of twelve miles or more. What a preparation there would be! It began the previous afternoon; after the day's ploughing the men who were to take the road groomed their horses with the greatest care, combed out their manes and tails, examined their feet and shoes, polished the harness. Others would have been called in from hedging to grease the wagon-wheels. One old wagon I remember particularly for its antique shape. Yet it was as good almost as on the day it was made. Its wheels were mounted on wooden arms, bluish-black with generations of greasing, the colour, rather, of that mark made by the skidded wheel which used to be such a feature of the hills of the old Macadam roads; and smooth and hard and metallic-looking like that. 'Not before it was wanted, neither,' they would say as they smeared on the yellow grease with a stick and slid back the hub cushioned on it. The one thing that must not occur, the extreme of disgrace for a carter, was that any of his wagon-wheels should 'shriek', as they said; so much more indicative of the stigma of cruelty by neglect than the word 'squeak'. The feeling of a carter announcing his progress through a village by the shrieking of one of his wheels, before whose every inhabitant it would conjure a picture of a slovenly farm-yard full of things broken and neglected, stables dirty, horses badly shod and everything done correspondingly without forethought, can be imagined. Not only did the wheels need to be greased, but part of the locking device under the carriage; and though this might not make a noise, at a halt any other carter, innkeeper, or smith would notice it in a minute by the steely polish on the wood.

Meanwhile the barnman, with an assistant, was weighing and tying up the last of the sacks, and wheeling them to the threshold of the barn. Even in so seemingly simple a matter as the tying of the mouth of a full sack there was a right way of bunching the loose material and getting it tied in a sort of half-bow right close to the corn. I have seen the barnman impatiently flap the loose bagging of a sack tied by a weak-armed or careless lad, undo it, heave the whole thing up, punch in the shoulders and re-tie it. The difference in ease of handling a compact weight and a loose sagging one must be tried to be realised, and all these points were designed to save labour; as also the tying of a bow which could be undone in a moment.

Then the wagons were backed to the barn-door, two fifty-six-pound weights were laid side by side on the ground behind the wagon. One man—the carter—stood in the wagon, three men below, and one with a sack-barrow in the barn. He brought a sack and stood it on the weights; two of the men grasped it by the bottom corners and joined their other hands under its middle. (Sacks and pigs are loaded in the same way; only with pigs the ears take the place of the bottom corners of the sack.) At a common impulse they hoist and swing the sack up; its edge lodges on the back edge of the wagon, and at once, without losing the impetus of the swing, the third man must add his weight, pushing the sack upright from the shoulder. Then the carter takes charge and disposes of the load as he requires. This goes on until the bottom of the wagon is full of upright sacks in two rows; then one of the men below joins the carter, the man with the barrow stops and does duty as 'third man' in the hoisting up, and the two in the wagon in their turn heave a few sacks up to rest lengthwise on the shoulders of the upright ones. This makes up the load to capacity and also makes a kind of ridge roof of it when covered with the cloth—makes it, as they say, water-shooting.

Thus the wagons were left overnight, loaded and covered. Next morning by three o'clock the stables would be glimmering as the carters baited their horses; then they led them out into the wintry dark and backed them between the shafts by lantern-light. One candle seems little enough by which to accomplish all this adjusting of traces, breechens, and back-chains, yet they hardly needed that; knowing instinctively where they laid a hand on a hook and where they had to stretch out another to grasp a chain to draw over it, feeling the tension and the number of links hanging free. 'The third ringle,' one would call to his mate at the other shaft, and he would adjust the collar-chain to the third 'ringle' so that the pull was equal.

The carter had on his better coat, scarf, and cap, and there was a preoccupation and quiet solemnity over him since the previous evening, as of one on the eve of a long and important journey. The hames sticking up above the collar of the shaft-horse now become pegs on which each man hangs his greatcoat, basket, and all that he needs on the way. Then, long before light, they are off with their loads and their teams.

So they go, mostly walking and keeping an eye continually travelling backward and forward from the head of the first horse to the back of the wagon—sometimes for a short distance riding perched just under the front of the body. And the carter's thoughts travel to and fro, also, with his eye—the security of the cloth where the wind whips at it, the corn beneath; he sees it through cloth and sacks, the colour of it and the quality, standing out in bright, individual grains as when he took a layer of it upon the barn shovel and looked at it in the light of the doorway a day or two back, when it was being sacked up. He sees the field it came from, from the ploughing to the harvest—the old dispute once again revived during that ploughing, whether on that particular field it were best to plough deep or fleet for wheat. The ploughman, thinking of his horses, would say fleet, as

28 BARDAN FARM NEAR BRADFORD-ON-AVON, WILTSHIRE

29 BREWER STREET FARM NEAR BLETCHINGLEY, SURREY

a rule; but he knew in his heart that deep ploughed and well rolled was the best, because look at the crop last harvest, for which it had been ploughed deep, compared with that of three years back when the ground had been only just turned over.

The horses: he watches in the early daylight the chestnut mare his master bought last Michaelmas; how well she goes, steady-pulling, neither too free nor lazy, the steady tension of the traces bears witness. He considers how it was she was sold by her last owner, because, it was said, she would not get in foal. How he had met by chance on such a journey as this the horse-keeper who had had charge of that very mare, and how he had discovered what he had suspected, that a certain tiny plant grew in the vicinity of that place which, being given to the mare at the moment of the stallion's service, prevented her getting in foal. 'Do you reckon if she and the horse had been left alone in the field . . .?' he'd suggested. And how the man had looked! 'Well,' the chap had said in the end, 'if she'd got in foal I shouldn't have had her to work no more; I'd have been given another instead—and she were a good mare to work.'

He thinks back then, to the time when he had been a young man trying to drive a kicking horse to market, and how an old horse-keeper had given him some drops to put in the horse's ears which made her go quiet as a lamb. . . .

He passes a village in which the lit windows have a waning look in the spreading outer light; faces peep out, hearing such early traffic, and he meets men starting out to work. Then a less familiar country spreads out before him, a country seen only on such infrequent journeys; and he becomes absorbed in that.

Arrived at the town, and having delivered his load, he puts up his horses at an inn and has his dinner there. Afterwards he does a few small errands for his master, his wife, a friend; and starts home again. He arrives with his lantern alight as when he started; the village he passed where they were going out to work he has passed again just as the men were going in through the lit cottage doorways to their tea. He is not the same solemn, preoccupied person who started out; now he is flushed though tired, and full of hearsay that he is eager to tell.

So too in harvest, the stacker, who sits up there on the stack waiting for another load, staring into space. 'Whatever do those chaps think about?' a stranger said, observing him so immobile and vacant-looking. I knew just what he was thinking of; he was wondering whether he had made the stack-bottom big enough after all; he was making complicated calculations of how many hay-cocks had gone to that load they were just finishing, judging it by the distance the wagon had traversed in the loading; and therefore how many more loads the remaining cocks represented, and when he ought to begin topping up the stack, and if they didn't finish to-day how much the stack would sink so that it might take another load and more perhaps to top it up again; and however he was going to keep that corner right with this wind blowing right on to it. . . .

The thatcher on an autumnal morning looks round the full rick-yard. He works at so much (it used to be two shillings) a 'square'. Not being good at arithmetic I only after years arrived at an estimate of what a 'square' was—their number is ascertained by measuring the length and breadth of the stack at the eaves and then doing sums which the thatcher is expert at. But this morning, with a shrewd and merry gleam in his eye, he says, 'Now see here, master, so as you be willing, I'll do a deal with ye—I'll take so much to thatch the lot, and no measuring up.' The master, being thus challenged to a battle of judgment, takes a long look round, considers, and says after an attempt to bid him down, 'All right, I'll take ye.' And each goes off secretly elated at having gained an imagined small advantage. And many times later each will have another long look and wonder whether the advantage has been theirs or no, thinking sometimes the one and sometimes the other. And neither of them will ever really know.

The cowman's anxieties are for the meadows—what fields are to be cut and what to be fed; while the shepherd is quite apart in his view of the farm. The farm, he considers, is for the sheep. In a drought he grows more and more suspicious of every stranger that comes to the farm, for he reckons he has come to try and buy that bit of kale by the side of the road, the only good bit of feed for miles around. Once, a shepherd I know of was accosted by a man he knew as such a buyer, asking if his master were at home. 'No, he ain't at home,' he said. 'Then perhaps the missis is at home and I could see her.' 'No, she ain't at home neither.' Unfortunately, just at that moment the master appeared in sight. 'Ha,' cried the man, realising the shepherd's cunning, 'you thought you'd give me the buck.'

'Ay, seeing as I know what you come for—you come to try and buy that bit of feed. I know—I see'd you looking at it often as you've been riding by.'

'You're right, and I reckon I'm going to get it.' And he did. He offered such a good price that the farmer was tempted beyond resistance. It was particularly hard on the shepherd, as it was he who had urged his master to break up that former rough little field and set it with kale. His advice had been too good. His master bought off his wrath only by a bonus on the sale of the feed, and the promise of handsome recompense to the sheep.

The shepherd, whose cottage is almost among the farm buildings, always has an eye to see if the master has a visitor in the evening. They will pass and the master will call out, 'We're going to have a look at the sheep after tea.' So after tea the shepherd is standing in the fold, and, as the master and his friend lean over the hurdles, urges the sheep gently so that they pass before them. He stands absolutely impassive, only speaking if spoken to, gazing at the sheep as though they were so many stones, yet straining for every word that the visitor may have to say.

This organism of the great farm, with its intensive cultivation, individual specialisation, its use of machinery in alliance with hand- and horse-power, I should call modern as against later tendencies which must be classed

31 INSIDE THE FAMOUS BARN AT GREAT COXWELL, BERKSHIRE

32 THE GREAT MILL ON THE KENTISH STOUR AT STURRY

as modernist. For the modern farm is based simply on production, while many modernist changes are an attempt to cope with economic distortion. The running of sheep on sound arable land turned down to indifferent grass, the corn-farming by chemical fertilisers and harvester-threshers, are only a sort of self-defence by low farming and still lower costs.

The big unit of four-course-shift cultivation fell to pieces rapidly after the war, and has only in its last hour been held together precariously by State subsidy in one form and another. Meanwhile the problem of the small cultivator remains much what it has been. In the days of prosperity the family farm of one hundred acres or less was primitive in its life; it was work from dawn till after dark every day, with the isolation that comes of lack of leisure. But it was only the first stage in a family ascent in the scale; the sons would become employers of labour and even end as large farmers. To-day the family farm is neither up nor down—it just exists by not spending, by having no labour-bill. On the other hand, in the grass country of the west a greater sense of leisure, or at least a less acute preoccupation with the working of the soil, makes individual independence seem less an exchange of one master for another. Here a man with a cow, a few sheep, a cider orchard, and several rods of garden ground on which he may grow roots for his cattle, is tolerably content. He is free to go to market, where perhaps he will do a little deal that will pay for his day's outing, and he sees his friends. His life, pivoted on his own axis, has not the epic quality of the community of a big farm, but no one can give him the sack, or say, 'I shall want your cottage at Michaelmas for another workman.' His interest in things is less technical, more personal and social, than that of the worker on the big farm; he is less in the grip of the seasons than his arable counterpart.

I have in mind a small west-country farmer, a dark-haired, dark-eyed, wiry, merry man. His leisure, his sitting for ten minutes to take a pint of beer, is dynamic, not a dazed lapse into lethargy. His mind is working and leaping. He keeps dairy cows and store cattle, his river-land costs over three pounds an acre to hire; it is too strong for cows in milk; it will fat two bullocks per acre. He also does motor-haulage and he loves the hills. The hills are a perpetual challenge to him; he likes to recount how he has taken his vehicle down places where people thought no vehicle could get, and then how he has got out of them again, loaded. How he came down one narrow, winding hill of extreme steepness backwards, stopping every so many yards to unload sand. One day he recalls, when he had to go to Bridgewater and the road was flat, he could see the country for miles ahead. He hated that, he hated to see just where he was going to; he nearly died of dullness. What he liked was a corner every few hundred yards, a hill, and then some new view. Though he has lived all his life in his steep valley, he loves the country—and he continues to see it consciously with his eyes—and the beauty of it—not just instinctively to know it. And then, in the harvest, more hilly feats; carting hay with the loaded wagon at an angle of nearly forty-five degrees, and an extra horse pulling on the load, pulling obliquely uphill to keep the whole thing from toppling over. And how once, when a load did turn over, they got the horses to pull it up again, with the load still roped to the wagon. And how, in the evenings, the people of the village who weren't farming people—the blacksmith, the carpenter, shoe-maker and such-like—used to come into the hayfield after their day's work was done and help with the hay, just for the sociability and fun of the thing, and for being in the big tea- and cider-party in the field later on.

In the arable country they call grass-farming 'lazy-man's farming'—with visions of every day that walking round to have a look at the cattle which they indulge in on Sundays. The grazier, no doubt, would modify the picture considerably; while the dairy-farmer's life has become an affair of monotonous time-table regularity. Gone are the days of cheese-making and butter-making, at least on the scale to which they used to be practised. How many farm-houses to-day have, as they used in the Cotswolds, cheeses maturing in the cheese-rooms under their stone-tiled roofs, till the day of the cheese-fair, when a wagon cleanly strawed was drawn up below and the cheeses let down into it by means of a pulley? It is easy, perhaps, to exaggerate the effects of these changes by the sentimental attraction of old customs; but what cannot be exaggerated is the loss of the stamp of in-dividuality in every product of the old life. By a mys-terious attribute each farm's cheese, butter, cider, had its individual characteristic. Some slight difference in recipe accounted for it partially, but not wholly. In some families a recipe for cider would be handed down from generation to generation.

Towards the borders of Wales, where the urban influence is less strong than in the Home Counties, and where the hilly nature of the country makes wholesale methods impracticable, the small occupier continues to exist as one among an equal society of small occupiers. Often he combines farming with some village trade. Generations of servility to a master have not induced that dazed and fatalistic mood which so often one meets with in the landless employee. One feels about the latter that with all his knowledge of the soil and its management, his technical skill, and real goodness of heart, there is something paralysed in the very centre of his being, so that he does not know, in a sense, what he knows, or that he can do what he can do. He is fearful of making a decision, and says no, he doesn't think he can do such and such a job, and then goes and does it perfectly. The small occupier does not keep the best stock; he does not as a rule farm in the most productive way; he patches up and makes do, he does not launch into experiment, but this central part of him is free, and all men are his equals. This must not be taken as favouring land-settlement in small-holdings for an urban surplus. The small farmer is a product of many generations in one place; without his intuitive knowledge of the ground he occupies he would not last a year. And how many from a town could ever manage to beat a piece of iron into a shoe and so save a blacksmith's bill, or make an ash-pole do to replace a broken shaft? It is not too much to say that half the small occupier's success is in power of transforming what is to hand into something that will serve his purpose, whether it is hedge-poles or a heap of old iron. This, of course, is in the direct line of our home-made rural culture.

Each district, with the scale and kind and quality of farming peculiar to it, reflects the extraordinary diversity of this small patch of earth called England. What could be more contrasted than the Fen Lands, where they go down on their hands and knees to the soil, the modern fruit-farms where hosts of men and women work together, with the lonely sheep-walks of the moors and downs and fells? Or the model farm and hunting-box of the Midlands, where the hedges are like garden-hedges and as though put there for horses to jump over, with the cottage-farmer of, say, the Wye Valley, with his patch laboriously cleared of boulders? In one spot we see the harvester-thresher cutting a thousand acres of corn, in another a man with a scythe mowing his steep half-acre; in one field a gyro-tiller at work, moving the soil like water, in another only a few hours distant a man guiding a single plough round a rock.

Nowhere, perhaps, do ancient and modern still consort together so curiously. Everywhere you go agriculture is a picture of the ingenuity of man in adapting himself to the place in which he finds himself, and a reflection of an inherited body of experience.

65

Charles Bradley Ford

THE
VILLAGE

FOR over a thousand years the village has formed an integral part of the pattern of English life. If on the whole it has developed consistently in response to the needs of economic evolution, in the process its outward forms have remained obstinately unstereotyped. The pleasant varieties of these that survive, briefly touched upon in later pages, provide a field of study that could well in itself exhaust the allowance of this chapter. But to the thoughtful Englishman the subject holds deeper implications. Beyond the loveliness which is its inheritance, which the accompanying photographs well show, is the immense importance of the village as a unit of national development, a cell that has given strength to the tissues of a widespread later growth.

A village life of sorts is developed by most primitive peoples with the rudiments of an agricultural economy. That it found an early footing in this country is evident

33 A COTTAGE GROUP ON THE TRENT NEAR WAREHAM, DORSET

34   A VILLAGE OF THE STONE BELT: WADENHOE,
NORTHAMPTONSHIRE

from the reconstruction of such a settlement as the Glastonbury 'Lake' village, raised up on stilts some 3,000 years ago above the peat-swamps of Sedgemoor; that it developed on organised lines appears from such village remains as those at Woodcuts Common in Cranborne Chase, Wiltshire, which are roughly contemporary with the events of the New Testament. Each reveals a standard of life not inferior in its way to that prevailing in Western Europe at its period, and suggests a fairly settled if still primitive type of peaceful community, whose level of culture can be gauged from a considerable range of excavated craftsmanship. In the early world the existence of such communities was governed by the imminence of the great invading migrations, whose waves broke successively over English soil, carrying with them all but the most obstinate traces of primitive culture and endeavour; and the village as we know it to-day has no roots in history deeper than the Saxon age, when a people wearied with the labour of conquest settled down again to husbandry in the forest and moorland clearings of a primeval England.

Field, ing, ham, hurst, tun (ton), these are still among the most familiar of our place-name suffixes. Their occurrence may be taken as a fairly accurate indication of the Saxon origin of a village; and it is an exciting thought that many of these quiet settlements, caught in the net of the English lanes, have in fact existed continuously by the fieldwork of their inhabitants for 1,500 years or more. It may be assumed that the first centres of conquest were quickly multiplied. The son or servant of a theyn would receive permission to make his own clearing, where he would build a loghouse, much after the manner of the backwoods settler of our own times, later adding outhouses and surrounding the whole with a stockade that raised it to the status of a *tun*. This suffix, preceded by the settler's name or other descriptive phrase, might well be adopted as its name; Ednaston, for instance, is simply *Eadnoth's tun*, and Pyrton means the *tun* of the pear-trees. In these far days the place-names are one of our most intimate approaches to the topography of Saxon colonisation. At Tubney in Berkshire one Tubba must have established himself on an islet of firmer soil among the marshes of the upper Thames; Nettlebed has remained explicit through the passage of fifteen hundred years; Wednesbury (*Woden's hill*) commemorates the worship of the Germanic gods. We know little of the life of these places save that it must have been self-contained and intensely isolated. Their organisation remains debatable; we shall never know whether the English villager is more largely descended from the free cultivator of a self-ordered community or the hereditary bondman of an absolute master. What is certain is that in the dark era of Danish invasion that followed the small man was often glad enough to bind himself to the more powerful one by ties of service in return for the protection of his life and property; that in practice if not in theory the manorial system spread increasingly through this island in the centuries that preceded the Norman Conquest (though free villages seem to have remained, particularly in the Danelaw and

in the South-west); and that it only required the consolidation of that conquest in the twelfth century to
forge into legal fetters the 'customary' bonds of the
English serf and slave.

If in these days it is part of most liberal theory 'that
the land should belong to the people', in the centuries
that followed the Norman Conquest it was certainly the
fact that the people belonged to the land. While agriculture to-day is one great industry among many dependent on private enterprise, in the twelfth century it was
the almost universal occupation of Englishmen, noblemen or commoners, bondmen or free, conducted on
age-long co-operative lines over a vast system of self-
contained and self-supporting units: the manors. We
may surmise that the substitution of a Norman lord of
the manor for a Saxon theyn had meant little alteration
in the machinery of the system save for an inevitable
tightening up of its cogs, the forcible reduction to
bondage of many who were free, and the carving
out of more manors from the rough unreclaimed lands
and far corners of the realm. Possibly the timber
homestead of Saxon days would be replaced by a
stone hall or keep, placed among barns, sheds and
dovecote in a courtyard surrounded by a stockade
and ditch; and the Saxon chapel by a sturdy little
stone structure of two or three cells, perhaps apsed,
with an imposing and grotesquely carved south doorway.
Adjoining this group, and rather in the same relation
to it as the huddle of negro cabins to many a planter's
house in the American Southern States, would be the

village—at the time of which we write probably a tumble-down collection of some thirty or forty one-storey hovels built of mud, but each with its toft, or small patch of fenced or hedged-in garden. The ways between the huts would be thick with mud and offal; beasts would wander in and out of the cottage doors at will, and from holes in the thatch smoke would issue in thin, peat-pungent curls. One cottage would show by an extended pole that it was licensed to brew and sell ale; a more important one would probably house the bailiff. A small mill with turning water-wheel would be recognisable beside the stream, and, passing between the houses, would come perhaps a warm gush of baking from the communal ovens.

Adjoining the village lay the common fields, three broad expanses of arable that were farmed in yearly rotation, the first sown with wheat or rye, the second with barley and the third left fallow. When you came closer you would see that each of these was patterned by the plough into a tangle of narrow strips, separated one from the other by turf ridges or 'balks' (which, with the 'headlands' or untilled spaces left for turning the plough, are the precursors of many of our twisting lanes and field-paths.) The three fields constituted the arable portion of the manor farm-lands. In them each bond-man or villein, bound in hereditary service to the lord, was endowed with his own yard-land or virgate of some thirty acres, though there were also half-virgate men who would farm about fifteen. The virgate was no compact holding, however, but the sum-total of a group of acre or half-acre strips scattered among the fields by a complex and apparently indiscriminate system of apportionment, mainly with an eye to ensuring the equality of each man's portion.

In addition to the ploughed fields you would notice, stretching away beside the stream, the common meadow, in which each man pegged out his yearly portion by lot, which he would fence off with hurdles before the hay-harvest; at other seasons he must lay it open as pasture. Away above the village would lie the 'waste' on which all had equal rights of snaring, turf-cutting, wood-gathering, pasture—a real stretch of the primeval England, this, whether the gorse- and bracken-covered 'common' that we know to-day, a piece of virgin moor or down, or one of the shaggy expanses of scrub and bent that the centuries have tamed into their present quiet chequerwork. The real woodland and forest, thick and impenetrable beyond anything we know to-day, was generally reserved by the lord for his hunting, though on payment of a 'pannage' due of, say, a penny a pig the villager could buy right of access for his beasts at certain seasons to fatten there on beech-mast and acorns.

Scattered among the strips of the common fields was the lord's demesne, or home farm, though this may have been occasionally in part a compact holding. The system of villeinage hinged on the cultivation of the demesne by the virgate-holders on fixed days of the week, usually three in number, together with the payment of certain dues in money or in kind, according to a schedule which represented the 'custom' of the manor and varied considerably in different cases. In return, the villein was allowed to consume the produce of his virgate, to which, however, he was bound for life by the conditions of his servitude, the land on his death devolving upon his eldest son, though in some districts, rather curiously, the youngest son inherited. By a tyranny common to all Western Europe at this time, the lord (whether he were the king, a monastic community, or simply a gentleman living on his own land) had absolute rights of proprietorship over the villein and his possessions except to maim or kill; there was no higher court, no appeal. Nevertheless, these rights were in most cases wisely modified by traditional usage, often stronger in itself than written law; and though theoretically a villein could be removed from his land or even sold outright with his brood at the caprice of his master, in practice his tenure of it was often just as stable as that of the lord himself—more stable, in fact, at the turbulent moments of medieval history. More, in the manor court which dealt with all except ecclesiastical disputes and offences, the villein was not only entitled but compelled to participate as a juryman, while his own elected reeve (a job that can seldom have found a willing candidate) was often required to organise his labours under the supervision of the lord's bailiff. These labours were ordered by an age-long and unyielding routine that realised a meagre substance for months of unremitting toil. The co-operative nature of the work precluded development or experiment; as a unit, the villein was hardly more important in the scheme of things than the pair of oxen which, as full virgate-holder, he supplied to the team of eight that dragged the unwieldy manorial plough. At no other stage of agrarian development has the cultivator been so closely identified with the land, or his life so regulated for its well-being.

If the villein or half-villein was the most numerous and typical member of the village community, there was a class of freeholders or *sokemen* mainly existing within the Danelaw which had managed to maintain its independence through the rigours of Norman Conquest, though its lands were usually intermingled with the common fields and its status little in advance of that of the bondman. A larger and humbler category was that of the cottar, bound in servitude to the lord but with a holding of a few acres in the common fields. His position might be described as intermediate between the small-holder and agricultural labourer of the present day, and he was usually required to work one day of the week on the demesne (Monday, hence his frequent title of *lundinarius*), though his services were most in demand at times of particular pressure such as harvest and sowing. The *servus* or slave became happily to a great extent merged in this class during the twelfth century. By the thirteenth he had practically disappeared.

Such were the principal grades of our village forefathers. Before passing on to the movements that led to the emergence during the sixteenth century of a comparatively free class of yeomen and tenant cultivators, it may be well to scrutinise more closely the detail of the old predial round, to set the merits beside the abuses and try to conjure up some picture of the ways of village life seven centuries ago. It was a small, a very small world, and often a dark one. With the first gleam of dawn the village labourer had to rouse himself from his straw bed, and, in coarse-woven tunic and abundant hood, make his way through the early twilight to the great bare fields where he passed the daylight hours. We can still see him in the miniatures of the time, stooping to reap and bind the sheaves beneath the outstretched rod of the reeve, his wife and son working beside him; sowing, with the slow, fine movements that have attracted artists from the anonymous scribe of the Luttrell Psalter to J. F. Millet; with his long ox-goad plodding patiently beside the team that drags the clumsy wooden plough down the stiff furrow. We can imagine the long procession of winter evenings in the smoke-filled hovel, with no light but the flicker of the open fire of peat or dung, to which family and beasts crowded alike for warmth, and surmise that the six hundred words odd of his vocabulary were still sufficient vehicle for lively evenings of story-telling and gossip, ending often enough, as we learn from the proceedings of any manor court, in high words and a scuffle, with a sore head the next morning, inside and out.

A schedule of 1266, setting forth the dues and duties of a virgate-holder on a Gloucestershire abbey manor, gives a good insight into the daily round at this period. According to the custom of the time the services are shown at their estimated cash value, though in most cases they were still certainly performed as labours:

35 FULBECK, LINCOLNSHIRE: THE VILLAGE STREET

36 IN SHAKESPEARE'S COUNTRY: WILMCOTE, WARWICKSHIRE

SERVICES OF A VIRGATE

A. B. holds one virgate of 48 acres (in the manor of Hartpury), with messuage, and 6 acres of meadow-land.

From Michaelmas till August 1 he has to plough one day a week, each day's work being valued at . . . . . . $3\frac{1}{2}d.$

And to do manual labour 3 days a week, each day's work being valued at . . . . $\frac{1}{2}d.$

On the 4th day to carry horse-loads (*summagiare*), if necessary to Preston and other manors, and Gloucester, each day's work being valued at . . . . . . $1d.$

Once a year to carry to Wick, valued at . . $3d.$

To plough one acre called *Eadacre*, and to thresh the seed for the said acre, the ploughing and threshing being valued at . . $4d.$

To do the ploughing called *bencherthe* with one meal from the lord *ultra cibum* at . . $1d.$

To mow the lord's meadow for five days, and more if necessary, each day's work being valued *ultra opus manuale* at . . . $1d.$

To lift the lord's hay for 5 days . . . $2\frac{1}{2}d.$

To hoe the lord's corn for one day (besides the customary labour), with one man, valued at $\frac{1}{2}d.$

To do 1 *bederipa* before autumn with 1 man, valued at . . . . $1\frac{1}{2}d.$

To work in the lord's harvest 5 days a week with 2 men, from August 1 to Michaelmas, valued per week at . . . . . $1s. 3d.$

To do 1 *bederipa*, called *bondenbederipa*, with 4
    men, valued at . . . . . . 6*d.*

To do 1 harrowing a year, called *bondegginge*,
    valued at . . . . . . 1*d.*

To give at Michaelmas an aid of . . . 3*s.* 3*d.*

To [pay] *pannage*, viz. for a pig of a year old . 1*d.*

For a younger pig that can be separated . ½*d.*

If he brew for sale, to give 14 gallons of ale as toll.

To sell neither horse nor ox without licence.

Seller and buyer to give 4*d.* as toll for a horse sold
    within the manor.

To redeem son and daughter at the will of the lord.

If he die, the lord to have his best beast of burden
    as *heriot*, and of his widow likewise, if she outlive
    her husband.

From the foregoing it will be seen that the villein
A. B. was a man of some substance, and it is easy to
understand that he could hardly have performed his
duties and cultivated his virgate (here of 48 acres) without the help of a substantial family or of hired labour.
The same document indicates some of the disabilities
under which he had to labour—particularly under the
lordship of a skinflint monastic house. Of these, *heriot*,
or the death-due of the best beast in the stall to the lord
of the manor, was one of the most unpopular. On the
same solemn occasion the Church also had its picking
and extorted the second-best beast by way of *mortuary*
(its *tithes*, or exaction of a tenth part of the produce of
each man's land, in money or in kind, provided another

cause of disaffection that rankles to this day!) *Tallage* was a kind of specious poll-tax levied by the lord when short of funds, generally on some large-sounding pretext of public obligation. *Merchet* was an unpleasant marriage-due on women, *leyrwite* the penalty for carnal incontinence in the same sex, and there were several more. Further, it was usually the privilege of the lord of the manor to reserve for himself the monopolies of brewing, milling and, less frequently in England, baking. Failure to make exclusive use of the manorial services would involve a heavy toll of the home produce or a fine at the manor court. Thus at Wrington in Somerset during the fourteenth century:

> Be it noted that each customary tenant, as often as he shall have brewed one full brew, shall give to my lord abbot [of Glastonbury, the lord of the manor] 4*d.* under the name of *tolcestre*. *Item*, each customary tenant shall give mast-money [*pannage*] for his pigs, as appeareth more fully in the Ancient Customal. *Item*, be it noted that the customary tenants are bound to grind their corn at my lord's mill, or to pay a yearly tribute in money. . . .

It may be remarked at the same time that medieval dues or fines were seldom extorted to the full. A demand for 6*s.* 8*d.* might well be settled as low as 6*d.*, though where the inability to pay was complete, distraint would often ensue with a ruthlessness that calls to mind Victorian Ireland.

This, briefly, was the servitude under which the

9

English peasant laboured for some six centuries. That there was a reverse side to the medal is evident again to anyone who glances through a representative collection of medieval pictures. The simple, rather childish humour of our forefathers often finds expression in its games—whip-top and bob-apple, dancing dogs and bears which would draw the rapt attention of a whole village, friendly (or less friendly) wrestling bouts, and the merry free-fight of village football. To the periodical 'ales' held in church nave or parish hall all would subscribe—and few would return from them quite sober; while the extra or *boon* labours at times of particular pressure were rewarded by small orgies of eating and drinking at the lord's expense (we talk of *beanfeasts* to this day). Then there were public holidays in honour of patron saints which might develop into quite considerable churchyard fairs, with booths, dancing and amusements, such as may still be seen occasionally in rural Ireland; while in the frescoed gloom of the building passed the heartening pageantry of the Christian year to bring its message of refreshment and solace to the peasant spirit. It would be foolish to suggest that there was not much happiness, besides sadness and fatigue, in these first villages, most of which must have emanated from the newly enlarged and whitewashed fabric that stood so finely on the edge of the houses, sending out its peal over field and common to remind the tired cultivator of the impermanence of his labours and the brightness of their reward.

The causes of the movement that, over a period of

centuries, removed the feudal shackles from the English villager and imposed their present patterning of quickset hedges over the English fields, are too many and too complex to be recorded adequately in this chapter. It must suffice to recapitulate what is history-book knowledge: that during the fourteenth and fifteenth centuries new forces began to undermine the old accepted principles of land-tenure and husbandry, while with the sixteenth began that long process of disintegration in peasant life that was only to reach its culmination with the passing of the Reform Bill of 1832, when a magnanimous State at last began to award the village cultivator a stake in the legislature as tardy and dubious compensation for his lost stake in the land.

It has been seen that as early as the thirteenth century the customary labours of a villein were regularly accounted at their money value. As the Middle Ages advanced, it became increasingly the usage for a lord to permit the commutation of these 'works', as they were called, for their cash equivalent when desired—a process, intermittent at first, which was to develop into a commonplace of village life, bringing into being almost automatically a new peasant category, the hired labourer —at first recruited mostly from the cottar class. With the steady rise in wage-rates that accompanied the fourteenth century, it became an increasing temptation to the villein to slip away from his home manor to seek a more lucrative wage-earner's livelihood elsewhere—a crumbling tendency that the depopulation and scarcity of labour following the Black Death turned into a landslide.

The same causes often rendered the cultivation of the demesne itself by grudging and expensive outside labour uneconomic, with the result that the home farm now often began to be leased *en bloc* to a tenant farmer, much as it would be to-day. Among such contributory causes, the disintegration of the manor during the fifteenth century is easy to follow. It is to belated attempts to set back the clock at this time that must chiefly be attributed the ferment of discontent that, for close on two hundred years, poisoned village life—of which the Peasants' Revolt of 1381 was an early and alarming symptom.

Other causes contributed to the discontent. The considerable profits accruing from the sale of raw wool were beginning to attract not only professional staplers but members of the landowning class and even farmers, who, faced with an apparent deadlock in agricultural conditions, found a ready solution in the enclosure of large tracts of land for grazing. The movement towards the consolidation of a man's holdings in the common fields by mutual interchange had long been encouraged, but it was another matter when the tenant farmer, as he now virtually was, reversed the usage of centuries and let the old plough-lands lie fallow as grazing for his sheep. The demesne as a whole now became increasingly given over to the same purpose. A wave of indignation swept the country, however, when less scrupulous landowners began to exercise an obsolete prerogative and enclose with hedges considerable tracts of the common waste, which by immemorial usage had formed an

38 KEMERTON IN THE VALE OF THE SEVERN, GLOUCESTERSHIRE

39 NORTON IN THE VALE OF EVESHAM, WORCESTERSHIRE

STUDLEY PRIORY, WILTSHIRE

essential factor in the livelihood of their tenantry. What was a scandal towards the close of the fifteenth century within the space of some fifty years grew to be a real menace to internal peace. Land that had previously given occupation to a hundred men or more could now easily be worked by a couple of shepherds and their dogs, and though contemporary indignation is apt to exaggerate the extent of the evil, there can be no doubt that much unemployment and misery ensued. Furthermore, the work of the monasteries in relieving the poor and impotent had been dealt its death-blow by the Reformation, with the result that an army of underfed vagrants and 'valiant beggars' was loosed upon the countryside, adding neither to the amenities nor to the security of village life. Despite sporadic attempts at legislation, and the considerable oppression of the victims, the evil continued, mightily denounced though it might be in Parliament and from the pulpit, in weighted prose and doggerel verse:

> The towns go down, the land decays . . .
> Great men maketh nowadays
>   A sheep-cote in the church . . .
> Commons to close and keep;
> Poor folk for bread cry and weep;
> Towns pulled down to pasture sheep;
>   This is the new guisel

If the Agrarian Revolution in its beginnings created widespread misery among the lower grades, it was responsible at the same time for the emergence of a new class of yeomen and 'copyholders' (as the tenant farmers

came to be called from the nature of their lease: a copy
of the entry in the manor customal)—men of substance
and standing in the village community, whose well-
being became a particular concern of Tudor policy.
The villein whose forebears, by slow accumulation and
interchange, had amassed a comfortable holding, now
began to appear in his true light as a tenant farmer, an
employer of labour on his own account and no doubt a
luminary of the local vestry committee. The yeoman
freeholder, again, flourished exceedingly, particularly if,
as was frequently the case, he had turned over his acres
to grazing. It is from this period (*circa* 1530) that date
many of our earliest and best examples of village building
on a substantial scale. Pleasant West-Midland places
such as Hodnet (Shropshire), Pembridge (Herefordshire)
and Norton in the Vale of Evesham abound in good
half-timber houses, occasionally touched with decora-
tive craftsmanship, built to two storeys and roofed with
tiles or thatch—houses that have served the needs of
generations of yeomen and small-holders from Tudor
times. Nevertheless, as customary labour continued a
legal if seldom a practical reality well into the next
century, so, side by side with the new houses, with their
great oak beams and gleaming plaster, must have survived many of the 'decrepit hovels, with rotten beams
and half-ruined walls' that had sheltered cottar families
for centuries past—places of the type against which
Bishop Hall inveighed as late as 1610:

> Of one baye's breadth, God wot! a silly cote,
> Whose thatched sparres are furr'd with sluttish soote

A whole inch thick, shining like black-moor's brows,
Through smok that down the head-les barrel blows:
At his bed's-feete feeden his stalled teme;
His swine beneath, his pullen ore the beame:
A starved tenement, such as I gesse
Stands straggling in the wasts of Holdernesse;
Or such as shiver on a Peake-hill side,
When March's lungs beate on their turfe-clad hide . . .

In certain well-favoured neighbourhoods the production of wool brought into being definite and delightful schools of village architecture. Of such were the
Cotswolds, where places as precious as Stanton, Stanway,
the Subedges, Willersey, Mickleton, began as early as the
fifteenth century to take shape from the resources of
the local stone and the considerable profits accruing from
the local wool. In such districts the spacious beauty of a
church, or the presence of a Tudor manor-house beside it,
testified to the altered circumstances of village life. The
transformation of the older, cramped fabric, patched and
altered over four centuries, into its ultimate beauty of
panelled stone and painted glass was effected, as often as
not, by the combined effort of the community; the new-
comer who pulled down the comfortless, forbidding little
fortress of the medieval lord was perhaps a shrewd and
cultured capitalist of the type of the Tames of Fairford
or the Spryngs of Lavenham, who substituted smooth
lawns and a fish-pond for the old stockade and ditch.
In the Eastern Counties, which from the dawn of the
fifteenth century had established themselves as the cradle
of English textile production, a further tendency was

apparent. Here many villages were centres of a specialised line of industry, of which the products often still
bear their names, as Worsted and Kerseymere. Kersey,
from which the latter derives, remains a lovely and
untouched example of the early manufacturing village,
with its street of gabled and plastered weavers' houses
climbing to a fine church. Boxford, Stoke-by-Nayland,
Glemsford, Coggeshall are others of the kind in this
district, and Lavenham, which some might call a town
and others a village, is loveliest of all.

But these are superlative examples. The average
village, which still, it may be noted, subsisted almost
entirely by agriculture, a little of it on the new system
but most of it by the old routine of open-field cultivation, developed much more gradually. In the bare,
rolling prairie that was England each of these small
places was of necessity a self-sufficient unit, for its
communications with the outer world, deplorable at the
best of times, were often impassable in winter, 'when
cheeks be nipt and wayes be foule'. An ingrained
tradition of craftsmanship made each householder the
artificer of his own utensils and tools, even down to the
spoons, bowls and platters of treen and the osier baskets.
Men tanned their own leather and built their own ploughs,
but the iron coulter, where it was used, was fashioned by
the smith, with most other sorts of simple metalwork
that required a fire and a forge. The womenfolk were
equally versatile in their sphere. A housewife had to
be able to spin cloth and linen for the family wardrobe
beside her duties in brewhouse, bakehouse and dairy.

84

41 A YORKSHIRE VILLAGE: CRAKEHALL AROUND ITS GREEN

A significant innovation of this time was the appearance of the first effective type of cottage lighting, devised by setting peeled rushes in a tallow bath. The gloom of the Middle Ages was pricked by the glimmer of innumerable village lights.

It was Elizabeth who, in the direct trend of Tudor policy, gave the village its first importance as a unit of local government. It was ever part of the home policy of that determined House to invest by degrees the inherent power and influence of the lord of the manor in the yeoman and farmer class, which it recognised as the first national mainstay both in peace and war. As the sixteenth century drew to its close the spread of pauperism and vagrancy increasingly demanded legislation, but the Elizabethan poor laws did more than cope with an immediate problem: they established English local government on a definitely parochial basis. While the royal authority was represented in every district by its appointed justices, local affairs were now largely conducted by groups of parish officials, paid and unpaid, but mostly elected by the free vote of the people.

It is only possible to record very briefly the principal categories of these officers who so largely controlled the conduct of country matters until the Industrial Revolution came to change once again the trend of English life. The churchwardens, though their function was largely ecclesiastical, were busier men than to-day, for besides supervising the upkeep of the fabric and its services, and keeping the church accounts, they were responsible for the presentation of moral offenders at the archdeacon's court, and collaborated with the overseers of the poor in the distribution of parish charity. The latter officials had to deal with the manifold problems of acute unemployment—apportioning the means of relief in money or kind, providing work where work was to be found, and caring for the destitute, young or old, of both sexes. To accomplish this a poor rate had to be levied and collected, and the overseer's path was often a thorny one. The surveyor of the highways had to wrestle with the almost hopeless problem of communications, which had fallen into appalling disrepair, particularly since the constructive work of the monasteries had ceased. Finally, there were a number of annual and honorary offices of which the names are often explicit, such as those of the well-master, the aleconner or taster, the alnager or examiner of broadcloth, the clerk of the market, and the hogringer, whose particular duty it was to see that all swine had rings in their noses to prevent rooting.

But of all the parish officials the most important was the constable, who was responsible to the justices for the maintenance of order in the village, the carrying out of warrants, the custody of offenders in his own house or the local 'pound', and, finally, the infliction of such punishments as whipping at the post or at the cart's tail, the stocks, the pillory and the ducking-stool, still much in demand for scolds and witches. The latter, seldom more than lonely or daft old women, were throughout the seventeenth century the objects of fanatical persecution in country districts, particularly during the Interregnum, when the blood-sport of witch-hunting assumed nauseating proportions. It may be added that the ladies often brought the trouble on their own heads by their eagerness to advertise their particular brands of potions and enchantments, though when, as rarely happened, one was committed to the Assizes, she was generally acquitted by a hard-headed town jury.

Though the seventeenth-century villager breathed a comparatively free air, he was still subjected to a degree of correction and surveillance in small matters that would seem intolerable even in Dora's England. The Tudor encouragement of archery was responsible for the pro-hibition of many of his time-honoured games, such as bowls, football and trippet, though James I, in his 'Declaration of Sports', reaffirmed his sanction of ales and morris-dancing. Drunkenness was severely dis-couraged, but flourished mightily, nevertheless, often behind the closed doors of the taverns, still marked by their distinguishing poles, now decorated with evergreen bushes where wine was obtainable. Village morals were supervised with patriarchal solicitude; yet despite the pinpricks of interference and the burden of rates he was often required to shoulder, the life of the cottager at this time was seldom a drab one. Mr. Bryant, in his *England of Charles II*, records such festivities as the Yule Plough, with its company of white-shirted sword-dancers, the Whitsun Lamb Feast, the Midsummer Eve wrestling, the popular bell-ringings, and the May Day games, 'when young men and maidens (who did not always return so) went out into the woods long before dawn to pick flowers and branches'. If the wages of the agricultural labourer were meagre, his menu, in farm-house kitchen or cottage parlour, was extraordinarily abundant and varied. England had indeed come to be 'a land flowing with milk and honey', and few of her sons failed to share in the plenty.

About the middle of the century a number of specialised industries made their appearance in village life to compete with the time-honoured occupation of farming. Thus, stockings were knitted by the cottage women of Gloucestershire, and woven in the villages of the Eastern Midlands. Looms whirred and clacked in the valleys of Devon and Somerset to supply the export trade of the western ports, and here also was produced a particularly fine white lace. Chair-turning had begun in the Chiltern Hundreds, but ironworking was beginning to move from its ancient centres in the Sussex Weald. The old communal self-sufficiency was no longer enough. The plenty of the English village was overflowing upon the outside world; its essential activities were forming the germs of new industries and enterprises.

The appearance of the village at the dawn of the eighteenth century had changed radically in the course of a hundred years; to the stranger from our own times it would indeed have come to assume a fairly recognisable mould. True, he would miss the comfortable Georgian miller's or doctor's house of brick, with its well-spaced sash windows and neat fanlight, as he would miss the pale brick or stucco school buildings of 1825 (or, worse, of 1865), and the Nonconformist chapel. But the main ingredients that we admire to-day would be there: the church, much the same on the outside at least, if a trifle shabbier and without its internal 'purification' of glazed tiles and pitch-pine; the range of almshouses, with its rows of gables and chimneys and donor's superscription above the central bay; the inn, with its scrubbed outside settles and freshly painted picture-sign. Some of the cottages, each still with its green toft, would be appreciably newer—but their design, except for the substitution of sashes for mullions in the windows, would be almost indistinguishable from the work of a century earlier, so hard does tradition die in the English Shires. It would be in strolling beyond the village that the visitor would recognise the most emphatic change. Despite the gradual encroachment of the hedgerow, England was still in the main a compound of shaggy waste and bare, strip-patterned plough-land, though the great estates were forming green islands of park in the unreclaimed stretches. Pleasant substantial farm-houses, surrounded by barns and outhouses, were also making their appearance, each the centre of a chequer-board of enclosed fields. Slowly the useless lands were dwindling from the face of England; less slowly the tide of population was rising in its village centres.

New activities were making their appearance in rural life. If the Court Leet still sat as a pale ghost of the manor court to settle the policy of agriculture in the open fields, as the eighteenth century advanced its decisions affected always fewer of the villagers, for the class of landless labourer was growing apace, resolving itself at the same time into recognised sub-categories which, at times of Mop Fair in the local town, could be seen assembled in groups for hire, each man displaying the emblem of his calling—the carter with whipcord in hat or buttonhole, the shepherd tufted with wool, the hedger with his bill, the field-worker with his shovel. For the first time also the tradesman was making his appearance in the village—a necessary as well as a lucrative appearance in most cases, for the state of the roads still isolated many communities in winter, and the trip to the town might be an ordeal as well as an adventure. By the middle of the century it was possible in a good-sized village to distinguish as many as eight separate callings beyond those directly connected with the soil or with the spiritual and physical health of the community: the innkeeper, the tailor and mantua-maker, the smith, the miller, the grocer, the butcher, the baker and the barber. At East Hoathly in Sussex at about this time a 'general dealer' could estimate his turnover at something like £5,000 a year, the equivalent of perhaps four times that sum in modern money.

If the star of the tradesman, the landlord and the more substantial farmer was in the ascendant, that of the labouring cottager was visibly waning. Much has been recorded of the material and cultural achievements of eighteenth-century history, but writers are apt to neglect what is surely one of its darkest chapters in this country

43 BLANCHLAND VILLAGE AMONG THE NORTHUMBERLAND FELLS

—the taking of its last lands from the poor and the sub-stitution of an undernourished drudgery for the plenteous activity of the older England. The story of the Enclosure Bills which, over a period of some seventy years of the eighteenth and earlier nineteenth centuries, withdrew millions of acres of the remaining waste from their time-honoured usage, to the great detriment and impoverish-ment of the labouring classes, should disgrace the resounding names of many great English families and perhaps bring a blush to the cheek of the Mother of Parliaments herself should she be capable of blushing. There is no space here for an examination of the complex legislative machinery by which these Private Bills, sealing the fates of communities from Land's End to Holy Island and from Westmorland to Thanet, were propelled from one bored and acquiescent Chamber to the next, finally to be put into execution by visiting commissioners against whose decision the villager had no right of appeal save by a Bill in Chancery. It must suffice that his last right to a use of the waste for his own profit generally vanished at this time. By Victoria's accession, save for such insignificant 'greens' and 'commons' as we know to-day, mostly of a poor soil that has resisted reclama-tion, England was ensnared in its hedgerow net, to the abundant advantage of the landowner, the farmer and the landscape-painter. The field-worker had sunk to a worse than feudal dependency.

From a material point of view, of course, there was much to be said for the new system, without which the immense developments of eighteenth-century agriculture could never have been effected; but if the experiments of a Townshend, a Coke or a Bakewell demanded a broader framework than the open-field system could have provided, the inclusion of the wastes in the scheme of things inflicted a gratuitous injury on a fine class from which it has never completely recovered. With the accompanying decline of wages during the eighteenth century, the village labourer had, by its close, sunk to a state of impoverishment and despair only comparable with that existing in 'derelict areas' to-day. Then as now the staple diet was bread and tea; but now at least there is the dole, and the 'unemployed' is not faced with the prospect of a tyrannical and pestiferous poor-house, to which many preferred starvation. 'Bully [Lord Bolingbroke] has a scheme of enclosure which, if it succeeds, will free him from all his difficulties . . .' so wrote Selwyn to Lord Carlisle, perfectly voicing the attitude of the landowning classes to a development regarded by them largely as a lucky windfall. It is little wonder that the youthful Dominions were fed with a steady stream of English agricultural labourers sentenced to incredible terms of transportation for rick-burning, hedge-breaking, machine-smashing, to say nothing of the 'crime' of poaching which supplied many an under-nourished family with an occasional square meal. The more organised disorders of 1795, 1816, and 1830, suppressed with a ruthlessness that shocked *The Times*, at least gave some publicity to the state of things, but with small avail. Such makeshift expedients as Speenhamland did little to ameliorate conditions, and the tide of population began to flow from the country to the new centres of industrial-isation, where a type of village was emerging in mining and spinning districts that we know only too well to-day. By the middle of the nineteenth century the villager had at least qualified as an object of Victorian charity; the plenty of Merry England was giving way to a diet of beef-tea and tracts dispensed by many a bombazine Lady Bountiful from her stucco-feudal bower.

Of course nineteenth-century benevolence was often of a better-directed nature. A new era of wealth was dawning for the landowning classes, who had invested the accumulated proceeds of centuries of agricultural effort in the industrial enterprises of the steam age, with the result that everywhere great houses were being rebuilt in the latest fancy of Victorian Tudor and Victorian Gothic, often with whole villages to match. The new mansions, with the lavish hospitality they offered, often constituted in themselves very substantial units of organisation and activity, and in such cases it was inevit-able that their villages should become to all intents and purposes dependent settlements, in which eighty per cent or more of the inhabitants were in the service of the estate. Given a good landlord the life of these places was tolerable and secure enough to those willing to display the outward subservience demanded by the new De Veres and Montmorencies. Real efforts were often made to improve housing and the amenities of village life, though all landlords were not so exact-ing as the Lord Pembroke who sought to replace alehouses by coffee-houses at Wilton, and rebuilt the respectable church in a surprising version of the style of Lombardy.

On the other hand, as the iron road cut its way through the new hedge-chequerwork, the country house, and the village with it, began to lose much of their former self-sufficiency. If near enough to London, the former could now degenerate into a mere base for occasional residence and recreation—and the largely absentee landlord was apt to be careless of his obligations. The chief trouble of most nineteenth-century villages was, in fact, their dependency on the rising and falling fortunes of landed proprietors. One might be a little paradise of hollyhocks, lattice panes and scalloped thatch such as Samuel Whitbread built at Old Warden in Bedfordshire; another might exhibit the worst signs of unkempt neglect through little fault of its own. Small country industries were fading, too, before the influx of factory-produced goods, and when the agricultural depression of the 'seventies descended like a blight over the land, while landowners could pull in their belts and live with fair comfort on their investments, it was often enough their tenants and dependants upon whom the burden fell, and the plight of many villages became unenviable in the extreme.

The long subsequent process of rehabilitation and administrative reform, culminating in Mr. Neville Chamberlain's Local Government Act of 1929 which restored a measure of its old importance to the parochial body, is rather outside the possibilities of this chapter. Nevertheless, the village as it exists to-day (excluding, of course, the purely industrial type, which is a village

45 BRETFORTON, WORCESTERSHIRE: THE CHURCH AND INN

46 SHERSTON: A STONE VILLAGE IN WILTSHIRE

47 JOHN BUNYAN'S VILLAGE: ELSTOW, BEDFORDSHIRE

only by the arbitrary gauge of population) poses some interesting problems. We may ask what is the material future of these often beautiful old places which the motor is bringing so quickly into the world again. The smithery is a garage and the inn a road-house with a Neon sign, and something of the same transformation is taking place within the community. That it *is* a community still anyone knows who has attended the meetings of the British Legion, Women's Institute or cricket club of a good representative village; but like most communities it is not particularly introspective, and becomes easily bored when told of its importance as a piece of social history, or of its environment as a thing of beauty. Its members will gladly exchange their creepered cottages for asbestos-tiled bungalows on the outskirts—and who can blame them, considering the comparative amenities of the two types of structure? As a thing of beauty the future of the village is certainly problematic, unless it is to be consciously 'preserved' as a setting for hand-looms and bright maiden ladies; its future in history brings us to the threshold of social and agrarian problems beyond the powers of our prophecy. We can only put forward our obstinate personal conviction that the village, as a unit of life and work, will not succumb easily. We have tried to show how closely its existence is interwoven with the progress of the English people; we cannot believe that such staunch threads are soon to be snapped.

．　　　．　　　．　　　．　　　．

There are ugly and nondescript villages as well as beautiful ones, but it is to the beautiful ones that we propose to devote our remaining pages. Their broad types are dependent on materials, which in their turn reflect the geological resources of different neighbourhoods. Of stone villages, for instance, most of the finest are to be found scattered over the limestone system which is the backbone of English geology. It covers nine counties, running in a rough diagonal from Portland Bill to the Humber, and comprises three outstanding village groups: the first embracing parts of Wiltshire, Dorset and Somerset, with Castle Combe, Montacute, Lacock, Biddestone, Cerne Abbas, Abbotsbury; the second ranging over Gloucestershire, Oxfordshire, Northamptonshire and Rutland, including the whole Cotswold constellation and moving north-eastward through Adderbury, Aynho, Colley Weston, Moreton Pinkney, Kingscliffe, Upper Hambleton; the third covering parts of Lincolnshire and East Yorkshire, with Fulbeck, Colby, Welbourne, Lockington, Bishop Burton. Other stone groups include the granite villages of Cornwall and the severe gritstone villages of the North.

The half-timber construction is of all, perhaps, the most widely distributed in this country, often appearing side by side with other materials. But certain districts have made it particularly their own: the Cheshire plain around Allerstock, Alderley Edge and Peover, for instance; the Vale of Evesham, with the Combertons, Elmley Castle and Norton; Southern Herefordshire, with Pembridge, Eardisland, Dilwyn; South-west Surrey, where Witley, Thursley, Chiddingfold, Eashing, wage a losing war against suburbanisation. If in many

Surrey cottages the timber framework is hung with rosy tiles, throughout much of East Anglia it is pleasantly faced with plaster, often tinted in light colours and occasionally enriched with patterned pargeting. The best group of East Anglian villages occurs at the junction of four counties—Suffolk, Cambridge, Essex and Hertfordshire—and includes Ashwell, Fulbourn, Finchingfield, Kersey, Cavendish.

Other varieties of fabric include the cob villages of Devon and of some of the Wiltshire valleys, the rather forbidding brick and flint of Norfolk, the weatherboarding of parts of Kent and Sussex and the usually undistinguished brickwork of the Eastern Midlands, ranging from the scarlet of the Pottery villages to the pallor of the Arlesey product; brick is also found as a filling for half-timber with good effect in several counties, particularly Hertfordshire, Hampshire and Berkshire. Roofing is an important ingredient of village beauty, and its varieties of complex distribution. Thatch almost invariably accompanies half-timber, and is also found in cob, plaster, and even some stone villages, as in Northamptonshire. The stone-slates of the Cotswolds weather exquisitely and give a final touch of distinction to their villages; roofing of much the same sort is to be found in West Yorkshire and along the Welsh Border. In some other parts of Yorkshire red pantiles are used, a picturesque later feature also to be found in Norfolk and the flatter parts of Somerset. But tiles remain the commonest covering for English houses—that is if we except the recent spread of blue slate beyond its native mountains.

Most English villages lie, for obvious reasons, beside a stream, and the hill-top village, a frequent Continental feature, is here something of a rarity—there was never the same need for defence. But a few may be mentioned in passing: Snowshill and Bourton-on-the-Hill in the Cotswolds, Priddy, lonely on the summit of the Mendip ridge, Kelshall and Therfield on the Hertfordshire chalk, Brill facing over to the Chilterns. Some of the loveliest lie in the shelter of an escarpment, as Stanton and Stanway beneath the Cotswolds, the Hagbournes, Hendreds and their neighbours beneath the Berkshire Downs, the group of Bledlow, Chinnor, Lewknor beneath the Chilterns. But the normal situation, as we have inferred, is more dependent on the economic requirements of Saxon settlement than on any strategic importance in the site. Where the land is good the villages cluster most thickly, almost one to the mile in some cases, as in the great vales of the Western Midlands and the softer stretches of Suffolk; similarly, in the bleaker parts of the country the village naturally seeks the fertile shelter of a dale, as among the Yorkshire and Derbyshire Pennines and the far-northern fells. But in ordinarily fertile country the distribution is apt to be haphazard, if generally pretty even. As the village community arose from the *personnel* of the manor, so its houses grew up on the site of the older settlement.

While certain elements go to the making of every village—the church, the inn, the stream or pond, the great trees, the one or two larger houses and the cluster of cottages in the local vernacular—their grouping is

48 A CORNISH FISHING VILLAGE: MOUSEHOLE

49 TOPCLIFFE, YORKSHIRE, BY THE RIVER SWALE

50 MATCHING, IN THE HEART OF RURAL ESSEX

of such capricious variety as often to add a spicing of unexpectedness to the pleasure of the effect. To cite a few instances, there is the village mapped out around a 'green', where small houses face one another across a half-mile of turf, as Ickwell in Bedfordshire, Fritton in Norfolk and Frampton-on-Severn in Gloucestershire. There is the village that spreads into several distinct clusters—one, perhaps, around a green of its own, another along a tree-fringed lane, a third centred round the churchyard or the pond. Composite villages of this type are Finchingfield in Essex, Hartest in Suffolk and Steventon in Berkshire—which, it may be added, are three of the most charming in the country. The 'combe' village of the West Country may be compared with the 'dale' village of the North; in each the houses are crowded into a corridor, the gardens clambering up behind their chimneys. Such are Mill Dale in Derbyshire and Melberby in Yorkshire, with the moors spread out above them, and the Somerset Holford and Horner in their orchard tangles. Some villages are built on either side of a main road, to their present advantage or disadvantage, whichever way you look at it; others are dangled off the main road at the end of a lane, and you have to turn your car to return to the world again. Some lie in a dip of hills or downs, with their church towers peeping above the crest, as West Dean in Sussex, Imber in Wiltshire and West Lulworth in Dorset; some fill a crevice in the cliffs, their houses rising in tiers from the water's brink, as Staithes and Robin Hood's Bay in Yorkshire and Boscastle in Cornwall. But the coast villages really demand a chapter to themselves, a chapter that will have to be written soon if it is written at all, for these places are, in the jargon of the speculative builder, full 'ripe for development'—a fate that has overtaken some and will overtake more.

No attempt to regiment the village into an ordered classification can succeed, because the charm of the English village lies in its fortuitousness, its happy sense of growing out of the soil with the trees and hedgerows around it. This harmony, the geologist will tell us, results from the use of indigenous materials in their proper setting, but there is more to it than that. The harmony of the village is in part an inward harmony, based on the Englishman's love of his soil and the house he has built upon it. Such freedom and content as have flourished in this country do still, notwithstanding many reverses, find their best material expression in the quiet beauty of many English villages.

G. M. Young

THE
COUNTRY HOUSE:
DOMUS OPTIMA

'EDWARD the Sheriff holds WILCOT. There is land for
10 ploughs. There are in demesne three ploughs
and six serfs. There are 37 villagers. There are 40 acres
of meadow, 20 of pasture, 50 of copse: a new church, an
excellent house and a good vineyard.'

From the edge of the plough-land, as you look over
the meadow, the copse, now a sanctuary for birds, is on
the right, the cotes of the village on the left. The house
and church are in their tuft of trees, and the thatched
wall, which runs across the middle of the picture, almost
certainly follows the line of the wall which enclosed the
domus optima, and the barns and yard where Edward
stored his crops, stabled his twenty-four oxen, and housed
his serfs. The church, indeed, like the house, has been
rebuilt more than once. But tradition still points out
the levelled slopes where the vines once grew, and in the

dining-room of the manor you may still see a fragment
of Edward's excellent house. No doubt it has rivals
in other places, though it cannot have many, because
Domesday rarely mentions a house at all. But, in its
own county, it is the oldest country house on record.

Standing as it does at the head of Edward's possessions,
it was, we must think, his chief and favourite residence.
A pleasant change it must have been from the dusty and
crowded lanes of the garrison city where he did his work,
and from which he took his surname, Edward of Sarum.
He had chosen well, or rather some far-off predecessor
had chosen for him, because Wilcot is the typical Saxon
settlement, with everything that a hungry, sea-worn
settler could desire. A spring-head of clear water, which
still runs past the Ford by the Wilcotes'; water gathered
in the great reservoir of the chalk downs and issuing over
the rich greensand at their feet; juicy meadows, easy
gradients for the plough, the best of turf for the sheep; a
bit of wood for the pigs, for fencing and fuel. He wanted
no more. But that he meant to have, and the English
landscape is, in its distinctive features, the creation of his
will. Later generations will enclose and improve; will
drain and hedge; will turn wastes into parks. But ultimately the Domesday landscape, *terra*, *pratum*, *pastura*,
silva, will be found underlying it all. When the Norman
came it had been five or six hundred years in making; it
reached its high point of pride and beauty in the middle
of the nineteenth century; and its mid-point everywhere
is the country house.

Edward's villagers probably spoke of The House, in

51 KNOOK, A TUDOR MANOR-HOUSE IN WILTSHIRE

52 MARKENFIELD: A FIFTEENTH-CENTURY FORTIFIED MANOR-HOUSE
IN YORKSHIRE

53 GIFFORDS HALL, WICKHAMBROOK, SUFFOLK: A MOATED TIMBER MANOR-HOUSE OF

distinction to the cotes in which they lived themselves. But all over England there is another word with which the Domesday commissioners must have become very familiar. 'The land belonged to four brothers, but there was only one Hall.' 'The Hall owns three horses.' 'Roger's land belongs to St. Edmund's Hall.' Generally, a hall is any house of outstanding size or dignity. In particular, it is the place where the collector calls for the King's taxes: the centre of the village economy; estate-office and court-house, and receiving-station for the local produce; where the corn is delivered and the reapers keep their harvest-home. To Shakespeare, a Midlander, Hall is the natural name for the great house of the neighbourhood:

> Kate of Kate-hall, my super-dainty Kate.

So it was to Crabbe, a Suffolk man, who wrote the *Tales of the Hall*; and to Tennyson, a Lincolnshire man, where

> Aylmer followed Aylmer at the Hall
> And Averill Averill at the Rectory.

In a list of Gentlemen's Seats of 1830 I find Hall and House in the proportion of seventy to sixty. Park comes third with twenty-five, and then Place. The significance of Place is something of a mystery. Park reflects the age of improvement, and the end of the days

> When Darnel Park was Darnel waste,
> And roads were all unknown as scurvy,

just as Abbey and Priory preserve the memory of the Dissolution. Anyone who finds himself, like Mr. Darcy of Pemberley, 'in his own house on a Sunday evening with nothing to do', and a gazetteer at hand, might perform a very useful piece of research by plotting the distribution of these names, and their relative frequency in different counties.

But how has hall come to mean a passage-way from the front door, a depository for overcoats and umbrellas? The answer to this question contains in brief the evolution of the English house, both great and small. 'The architecture of an old English gentleman's house was a good high strong wall, a gatehouse, and a great Hall and Parlour; and, within the little green court where you came in, stood, on one side, the Barn. They then thought not the noise of the threshold ill-music.' So Aubrey wrote in the seventeenth century, and his sketch of Bradfield Manor is both correct and typical. In the North, where

> Tarras and Ewes make nightly stir,
> And Eskdale forays Cumberland,

houses will long be built with good strong walls. In the South, where the King's peace is better kept, the wall need not be so high. Indeed, if you make it too strong, particularly if you provide it with battlements, the sheriff will probably call and invite you to produce your licence or to take it down. But, open or fortified, all houses conform to Aubrey's type of hall and bower, the hall for all purposes (unless you are so refined as to do your cooking behind a screen at the end), and the bower for the master and mistress to sleep in, and keep their few family treasures. As the world grows safer, and the gentleman, the yeoman, and the farmer richer, the bower develops at the expense of the hall, while the general adoption of the chimney makes it possible to ceil the hall and have a second set of chambers above. The hall, in fact, becomes, first, the central apartment of the Hall; then the entrance-room; finally the passage. Thus we end by using the same word for a vast complex of bowers and chambers, each intended for some specific purpose—eating, sleeping, reading, smoking, music, and billiards—and for a slip so narrow that a perambulator cannot get through without scratching the wall-paper.

But we are thinking now of the hall as country house, the home of the country gentleman, and if we look forward some four hundred years from Domesday we shall see that the country gentlemen have become the chief figures in a landscape out of which the once-powerful sheriff is beginning to fade. They are regularly invited to send representatives to Westminster to advise the King. The Boroughs are invited too, but unless a Borough is very independent—or very dependent—it will, as likely as not, ask some neighbouring gentleman to act on its behalf. The King's judges come down from Westminster to do the greater justice, but the lesser justice the gentlemen of the county will do themselves, in petty sessions and quarter sessions. It is, in fact, their position as justices that gives them their standing in the shire, and Aubrey, we find, will speak indifferently of a Gentleman's house, or a Justice's house. They have taken over the local adminstration; they will keep it till the Local Government Act of 1888; and they will not altogether lose it then.

What, in the meantime, has become of that manorial organisation of lord; villein, cottar, and bordar; free man and socman; which is depicted for us in Domesday Book? The form persists, and in the more primitive and dangerous North much of the reality. Everywhere manor courts are held to admit new tenants, to present defective hedges, tumbling walls, and blocked-up drains, and to fine the villager who neglects to put them right. But in the South the villeins are as free as their lord, and service on the lord's land has long been commuted for money rents. The lord is now rather the landlord, by the middle of the fifteenth century the lawyers can speak of *le lessour, appelé landlord*; he is the rent-receiver; and he may spend a year's rent, if he likes, on one splendid appearance in the tiltyard. In King Harry's days it will be a good investment for a young man of wit and muscle. What is more serious, he may pull down his cotes, turn a dozen holdings into one sheepwalk, grow wool for the Flemish market or make scarlet cloth for Venice, and put a hundred families on the road. Agriculture is becoming industrialised, and with the village economy, save as patron and magistrate, the country gentleman has less and less to do. In other words, the notion of farming for profit is making headway against the primitive practice of farming for subsistence, and where there is a growing urban or industrial area within reach—London, for example, or the cloth towns of the west—the profit is rapid and substantial. The distinction between the

Landed Interest and the Moneyed Interest is beginning to shape itself. But, as the actual cultivation of the soil is not yet scientific or progressive, the profit does not go back into the land. Some of it may go into merchant ventures, putting forth from London or Bristol. But more is spent in the building and decoration of houses, on clothes and horses, tapestry and furniture.

Typical of the age of transition in the fifteenth century, and a forecast of the age to come, is the figure of Thomas Tropenell and his manor of Great Chalfield. He was, we are told, and from the mask-like countenance and tight lips of his portrait we can believe it, a 'perilous, covetous man', and his chief occupation seems to have been the acquisition of estates with a doubtful title, which he then gripped fast. In his sixtieth year he began to enter up his title-deeds in a Ledger Book, which he continued till within a few months of his death at eighty-three, and which, after many wanderings, now lies once more in the great hall of the house which Thomas built. It is a defensible house, built against trouble from casual raiders or unsuccessful litigants, in a loop of the stream which turned its mill. The gateway and the walls were strong, but it was meant to be a comfortable house as well; with the noise and smells of the kitchen kept away; with parlours at both ends of the hall, and gallery and chambers above; and—strange contrivance—with pierced stone masks in the gallery wall, and in Tropenell's chamber wall, from which the ladies could watch the doings, and Tropenell could listen to the talk, in the hall below.

Soon, all over England, in the great peace which followed the accession of the Tudors, such houses were rising, on the site, very often, of the Domesday halls, or the dark and heavy Norman or Plantagenet houses which had replaced them. The fortified gateway became the lodge; the moat, if it was not wanted for swans, was filled up to make a garden. Light was more freely admitted and draughts more carefully excluded. The joiner, the carver, the stone-cutter, the painter, the silver-smith, felt the growing demand for their skill, and the broad windows began to glow with the arms of the family and its alliances, its friends and patrons, from one generation to another. They were built—or re-built—for the class to which Thomas Tropenell belonged, for gentlemen of blood and coat-armour, whose blood often becomes suspiciously thin when we have traced the pedigree as far as the grandfather. Now and then one of them shoots into fame and perilous greatness: a Cecil, a Seymour, a Dudley. But for the most part they do not aspire to rank. The great houses rise and fall, by battle, murder, and sudden death. The lesser families dig themselves in. They are satisfied to act as stewards to bishops and abbots and the great nobles whom they treat with profound and profitable reverence; to go once and again to Westminster as Knight of the Shire; to sit on grand juries; to pick up an estate here and an estate there; to marry their children well; to do justice and observe hospitality. They keep their land together; younger sons must fend for themselves, in trade or at the Bar, by a lucky marriage or a happy appearance at

54 WATER EATON: A SIXTEENTH-CENTURY MANOR-HOUSE ON THE CHERWELL, OXFORDSHIRE

55 BURTON AGNES HALL: A GREAT YORKSHIRE HOUSE OF THE EARLY RENAISSANCE

Court. They are constantly replenished, invigorated, and educated, by traders, lawyers, and courtiers who return to invest their fortunes in the land; and the dissolution of the monasteries provides the King with a vast treasure from which to reward their loyalty.

Once, when he was hunting, his horse pitched him head foremost into a pool of mud. He was pulled out by his yeoman, Moody. King Harry loved a Man, and indeed the service was one to command admiration as well as gratitude. Out of the forfeited estates of Malmesbury Abbey he gave him the manor of Garsden. The Moodys begin to go up in the world; they become, first gentlemen, then baronets. The fifth Moody, not liking the prospects for Puritans in 1640, sold Garsden to a Washington of Sulgrave, and retired to New England. Otherwise the successor of Yeoman Moody might have been summoned to Westminster Hall to sit in judgment on the successor of Henry VIII, because the gentlemen who in the fifteenth century had taken over the local government will grow so powerful, and so conscious of their power, that in the seventeenth century they will take over the royal government too. Indeed, one of them will some day be seen, and heard, walking in St. James's and putting the case to his companion: 'How if a man took on himself to be King?' Mr. Whitelocke of Fawley Court, Bucks, thought it would never do. Mr. Cromwell of Hinchinbrook was not so sure. To such a height will the country house rise, on the ruins of the monasteries, and under the patronage of the Tudors.

The sixteenth century is the decisive era in the evolution of the country gentleman and his home. 'The spring comes slowly up this way', but the breath of the Renaissance has fallen on the island at last. Of one great English house a foreign visitor wrote that 'it embodied the eternal craving of the North for the South'. In the houses of the later sixteenth century we can feel the touch of Italian science—proportion, balance, symmetry—working more and more powerfully on the transmitted Gothic instinct. The bowers arrange themselves more gracefully about the hall; a sense of mass and outline makes itself apparent now that the strong, high wall is no longer wanted. The E-house and the H-house emerge, as standard patterns, from the opening up of the 'little green court where you come in'. The smaller manors catch the feeling too, though here the Gothic instinct is more tenacious, and they show it in the more careful posing of the wings on either side the porch, and the poising of the gables above the windows. We are often aware of a certain youthful crudity, an exuberance of ornament, and trickwork even, on a homely background, in this Elizabethan and Jacobean blend of the Northern and Southern styles, just as we are aware of it in manners and literature. But a purer classicism is spreading among the patrons who commission houses and the craftsmen who design them, a freemasonry of taste and style which awaits, and will find, its accepted master in Inigo Jones.

As the country house under Elizabeth or James may be anything from a medieval manor, more or less adapted to modern standards of comfort, to a Renaissance palace, so the country gentleman may be, at one end of the scale, a cultivated and travelled man, a patron and a collector, and, at the other, a rough-coated, rough-tongued rustic. The one thing that unites them all is the consciousness that they are gentlemen, and that a gentleman is not made in one generation or two. 'I think, Sir William, you are of the Duke of Somerset's family?' 'No, Your Majesty, the Duke of Somerset is of my family.' They are the justices, they are the officers of the militia, and they are accustomed to be obeyed, if it be only by Tom carter and Dick shepherd, and in more intimate ways by Moll the dairymaid. But, allied as they are by marriage, occupation, and interests—the farm, the hunt, the muster, the bench, the grand jury, the county election—they are none the less divided. Most of them heartily accept the Elizabethan settlement of religion, and worship by the Prayer Book. But many families stand by the Old Faith, and there are others who think that the Reformation did not go far enough, who disapprove of bishops, and would not be averse to a new confiscation, this time of the bishops' lands. The future cleavage of Whig and Tory is beginning to make itself felt. But of more consequence, perhaps, is the distinction between those who have stayed on the land where they were born, getting such learning as they might need from the grammar school or the curate in the church, and those who have been to Eton or Shrewsbury, to Oxford or Cambridge, have kept their terms at an Inn of Court, have kissed their Sovereign's hand at Whitehall, perhaps have sailed to discover islands far away, or at least have swum in a gondola at Venice; who are not content to be the leading men in their county, but have caught sight of a larger stage for authority and display, at Court, on Embassies, in the Council Chamber, in Parliament.

With this we touch on a new idea—the notion of the country house as distinguished from the town house. Lords, spiritual or temporal, had often had their houses in London; Lambeth and Ely Place, Leicester House, Essex House, Barnard's Castle. But now, from the reign of James I, and with increasing rapidity, London is becoming a residential capital. We hear of Piccadilly and the Talk of the Town; we meet a young poet walking in the park, *suburbani nobilis umbra loci*, to admire the beauty of the London girls, and are, perhaps, a little surprised to recognise Mr. Milton, down from Cambridge. Indeed, the rapid growth of the new West End caused the Government some anxiety, and the Privy Council was obliged to intervene, to check unregulated building and to fix the prices in the more fashionable ordinaries. The Civil Wars did little to arrest a tendency which social circumstances made inevitable: whenever people have money in their purses they will go where they can spend it most freely; when they have not, they will go where they can pick it up most easily. Under the Commonwealth grave men were shocked by the display of horses and carriages, 'feathered men and spotted women', in Hyde Park, and could only record their satisfaction that His Highness at least was absent

56 BRYMPTON D'EVERECY, SOMERSET: THE GARDEN FRONT OF *CIRCA* 1660

57 WILTON HOUSE, WILTSHIRE, A DETAIL OF

58 MONTACUTE, SOMERSET: THE TUDOR PORCH

from these frivolities. When the King came back, even this consolation was lacking.

There is now a Town, and a Season, and at the end of the season the Town goes out of town to its country house, and the country house which had sheltered the dignity and expressed the pride of the great noble, the prosperous woolstapler, the successful lawyer, has begun to display and illustrate his refinement. Libraries have been formed; the portrait-gallery augmented by purchases from Italy and the Low Countries. Learned men are summoned to partake the hospitality and patronage of the great houses; craftsmen to adorn them. Soon England will be covered with masterpieces, great and small, the work often of unknown men who have learnt from Webb what Webb had learnt from Inigo, and Inigo had drawn from the fountain-head in Vicenza; unknown men, who could nevertheless, as part of their day's work, design a front that Sansovino might have approved, or throw out a cornice that Longhena might have envied. To carry the taste of Society into the country, to blend the elegance, refinement, wit, and activity of the metropolis with the old and dear delights, the sport and authority, hard drinking and hard riding of the country; in return, to bring back into Parliament, into public life, and into literature, something of the earthy and kindly vigour of the country, that is, historically, *testor lucos, et flumina, et dilectas villarum umbras*, the function of the country house in the days of Walpole and Fielding.

In creating this new function, the influence of London

and the example of the Londoners was perhaps the determining factor. Within thirty years of the Revolution the capital was ringed with houses reflecting the taste of King William in their gardens, and of Queen Mary in their chintz and china. Some of them were the houses of the nobility who wished to be near Westminster. But far more were the houses of merchants who wished to be near the Exchange. 'Very few of them,' Defoe wrote in 1722, 'are the Mansion Houses of families, the Ancient Residences of Ancestors, the Capital Messuages of the Estates; nor have the rich Possessors any Lands to a considerable Value about them. They are Houses of Retreat, Gentlemen's Summer Houses, or Citizens' Country Houses.' By 1750 the rush to the country was as marked a feature of a London summer as the rush to the seaside in 1850. Thirty years later Gibbon noticed that the fashion had spread to France, 'as a rural taste gains ground'. If it had gained ground a little earlier there might have been no French Revolution. The tidal inflow and outflow between London and the country, town house and country house, kept our social atmosphere sweet. It circulated wealth and improved communications. It diffused intelligence and manners. Above all, it created that large identity of interest between town and country, gentleman and citizen, landowner and manufacturer, which made Mr. Pitt the idol at once of the City and the country gentlemen in one generation, and made Sir Robert Peel, a manufacturer's son, the leader of the Tory party in the next.

The country gentlemen who could not live, or did

not share, this double life, sank, not indeed in their own esteem, but in the regard of the world. Formidable to their parson and their poachers, great men still to their farmers and copyholders, on a larger stage they begin to figure as Squire Western and Sir Hildebrand Osbaldistone; or, drawn by a kinder pencil, as Sir Roger de Coverley and Sir Everard Waverley. Lower still, the class for which we have no name, but which in Ireland would have been the Squireens, lives for us in Ensign Northington and Tony Lumpkin. Taken together, they form the bulk of the Stupid Old Tory party. The Whigs are definitely more fashionable, and, indeed, much of the parliamentary corruption of the eighteenth century came to little more than this, that an honest supporter who had swallowed his objections to the malt tax, or the employment of Hanoverian troops, was not above taking £500 from the whips with which to give his lady a season in London and his daughters lessons in music and drawing from the best master, or to replace the worm-eaten Stuart furniture with the latest designs of Sheraton and Hepplewhite.

The old style lingered on at Westminster till the Reform Act of 1832. 'Look at the loose, wide, brown coat, with capacious pockets on each side; the knee breeches and boots; the immensely long waistcoat, and silver watch-chain dangling below it, the wide-brimmed brown hat, and the white neckerchief tied in a great bow, with straggling ends sticking out beyond his neckerchief. He is a county member.' Very likely you could tell from his speech whether he sat for Norfolk or Somerset.

His son will be a county member too, but he will, in speech and attire, conform to the standards of his more refined age, and he will debate the Corn Laws on the principles of Ricardo, or lecture to his tenants on Liebig's Agricultural Chemistry, in the purest English that Eton and King's can teach. The squireens will last into the nineteenth century too, until the railways catch them and civilise them, and fashion bids them quit the flagged and mullioned manor of their ancestors for something out of Loudon's Villa Architecture, something in stucco, or in brick and slate, with a drawing-room and a hot-water bath.

Another turn is impending. The country gentleman of the nineteenth century is an administrative and scientific man. His grandfather, so far as he conformed to the ideals of his class, was an artistic, and particularly an architectural, man; commonly a connoisseur, often a student, sometimes a practitioner. An observation of Gibbs' admits us to a world of taste which had never existed before and was never to exist again:

'Some, for want of better Helps, have unfortunately put into the hands of common Workmen, the management of Buildings of considerable expense; which, when finished, they have had the mortification to find condemned by persons of Taste, to that degree that sometimes they have been pull'd down, at least alter'd at a greater charge than would have procur'd better advice from an able Artist; or if they have stood, they have remained lasting Monuments of the Ignorance

116

or Parsimoniousness of the Owners, or (it may be) of a Wrong-judged Profuseness'.

Towards the end of the eighteenth century the sense of pure design had begun to be confused by the growing taste for the Picturesque: the ruin, the hermitage, the awful grove, the solemn fane, the soaring pinnacle, and the enchanting vista terminated by a Gothick umbrello—or, quite possibly, by a Pagoda. Our domestic Palladian had worked itself out into an exquisite but sterile propriety; in turn the neo-Romanism of Burlington and Kent, and the neo-Hellenism of Adam had their day; and now the New Age was at hand, an architectual Bacchanalia of which Fonthill and Sezincote are the heralds, Barry's reconstruction of Highclere the proclaimed masterpiece.

> See: through the quiet land
> Rioting they pass,
> Fling the fresh heaps about,
> Trample the grass.
> Tear from the rifled hedge
> Garlands, their prize,
> Fill with their sports the field
> Fill with their cries. . . .

First Pointed! Second Pointed! Back to Elizabeth! Back to the Ages of Faith! French Gothic—Venetian Gothic—railway stations to look like Tudor halls, Swiss chalets brought down from their mountains to serve as lodges in the Vale of York, labourers' cottages vaguely suggestive of Nuremberg clocks, and parish schools intended to remind the cultivated observer of the tomb of Galla Placidia at Ravenna. This, the crowning example of Allusiveness in Architecture, may be seen at Milden-hall by Marlborough. For the rest, the curious may study Robinson's *Rural Architecture*, or visit Edensor.

The architectural sense had gone, but in its place the level advance of humanitarian feeling and science had imposed new duties on the country gentleman of the nineteenth century. His science was mainly directed to the improvement of the land, and his own revenue, by enclosure, drainage, and experiments in fertilisers and breeding. The standards of his class required it of him, and they required him also to be active for the housing, and, in alliance with the Church, for the education, of the people. I take at random the history of a small village, under a new and wealthy squire. He bought the property in 1828, and commissioned a pupil of Papworth's, James Thomson, to reconstruct the manor-house, which from sketches surviving would appear to have been a typical specimen of the symmetrical seventeenth-century style, executed in the local cornbrash. Under Thomson's hands it grew into something 'corresponding with the habits of refined modern society'. For our purpose, the dining-room and drawing-room, each 33 by 24 feet, 'with a large and lofty bay window to each', the library and the breakfast-room, are of less consequence than the treatment of the hall. It is still the central apartment, but it has been articulated into

'a range of halls and vestibules, each differing in their arrangement, but of a uniform character. The inner hall is octagonal and surrounded by a carved

59 BLENHEIM PALACE, OXFORDSHIRE: AN AIR VIEW OF THE GREAT VANBRUGH HOUSE

69. CHURCH AND MANOR-HOUSE AT WIDCOMBE, BATH

stone gallery, behind which rise tall, slender pillars
having ornamental capitals, whence open the ribs of
a coved ceiling and a lanthorn light. The vestibule is
terminated by an alcove, called the tribune. These
halls are fitted with Italian bronzes, and the tribune
is adorned by a beautiful statue of Venus Verticordia
executed by Gibson at Rome.'

It is the old union of Northern comfort and Southern
grace, but rendered in a new idiom.

'The gardens are surrounded by a wall one thousand
feet in length, covered on both sides with the choicest
fruit trees, and the farming houses include a pinery and
a vinery one hundred and eighty feet long, and exten-
sive melon pits. The stables provide accommodation
for a stud of fifty horses.'

Domus optima, vinea bona!

But Mr. Thomson was an expert in cottages, as well
as in stables and tribunes: cottages meant to be 'warm,
dry, and comfortable, and so more desirable to the occu-
pant than the village ale-house'. 'To each cottage is
attached a garden and a pigstye, and a most pleasing
effect produced in the habits and manners of their
inmates', that is, presumably, of the cottages. But the
whole parish felt the hand of the benevolent improver,
in the condition of its roads, farm-houses, hedges, and
plantations.

'Remembering what the parish was more than 60
years ago when the roads were almost impassable for

carriages in winter months, the labourers' cottages un-
fitted to protect their inmates from cold and wet, and
even the farm houses but little better, I cannot but
hail with much gratification their greatly improved
state to-day (1843). The farm houses with their appen-
dages afford comfort and almost luxuries to their
occupants, who are also provided with good and sound
roads for the conveyance of produce to the neighbouring markets: the cottages are provided with
water and drainage: every inhabitant has the privilege
of an allotment and the poor rates are only 3s. in the
pound.'

Go a few miles and see what you will find, in the mid-
fifties, at the peak of rural prosperity.

'The labouring population are very indifferently
housed. The dwelling rooms are few and small: the
sleeping accommodation is not decent: wells are
infrequent: the drainage is defective. The population
is decreasing. There are no pretty bridal customs,
and parents never think of gracing the union with
their presence. The same remark applies to games
and amusements: we have next to none. There were,
indeed, ten years since, the remains of a Michaelmas
revel, but the excise officers and the police stopped it.
We ought to be healthy, but it is no one's business to
drain the common. There, 17 children died of scarlet
fever in three months. The cause was patent: on the
common the soil is a rotten sponge which would
hardly bear the weight of man or beast. We have

the remains of an old pack road. The turn-pike is insolvent. The causeway is out of repair.'

And the reason?

'This state of affairs is no more than might be expected in a parish where the landed proprietors, being non-resident, want that interest in the people which would naturally arise from personal communication. The poor here are not neighbours to the rich.'

Two passages like these, placed side by side, furnish the clue to much Victorian history and still more Victorian declamation. A resident, unencumbered squire, *par negotiis neque supra*; progressive farmers; a village not over-populated, and furnished with pure water, good houses, allotments and a school, together formed one of the most successful experiments in social organisation that England had seen. The squire might be insolvent, encumbered, or an absentee. The farmers might be unintelligent. The labourers might be undernourished. There were many points at which the experiment could go wrong. But, when it went right, the country house did unquestionably provide a nucleus of culture and a basis of order and progress which nothing else could have furnished, and history must allow that when Prince Albert said,

'the country gentleman with his wife and children, the country clergyman, the tenant, and the labourer, still form a great, and I hope united, family, in which we gladly recognise the foundation of our social state',

he spoke no more than the truth.

Anyone familiar with our early landscape-painters must have noticed that though, as he goes about the country, he will constantly observe Crome skies and Constable cornfields, the broad spaces of De Wint and the tinted clouds of Varley, never will he see a village as they saw it. On the other hand, whenever he comes upon a cottage group which recalls a picture with figures, the chances are that the artist will be Birket Foster. Foster is pre-eminently the painter of that finished countryside, of that 'jewelled and enamelled neatness' which high farming under strict covenants had imposed on the vague and various landscape of the unscientific, unromantic age. We may regret that he was not a greater artist. But his merit and value as the recorder of an historic phase are not thereby impaired. His Quakerly blood, perhaps, gave him a particular interest in the landscape in which he grew up, in the industry, the regularity, the tidiness of it all; in well-ploughed acres and well-behaved children;

all thing in order stored,

whether in cottages or farms, or the glades and vistas of the halls which dominated and directed the farm, built the cottages and educated the children, and took their reward, as Johnson had once said, 'in money and homage'.

If one had to select the moment when the country house was at its apogee, one might take the year 1854, when Waagen brought out his *Art Treasures of Great Britain*. Prices were high, and the harvest the most

61 HACKNESS HALL: A GEORGIAN SEAT IN YORKSHIRE

62 THE MOOT, DOWNTON, WILTSHIRE: A 'MIDDLING' COUNTRY
HOUSE OF *CIRCA* 1680

Plate 13. STONE BUILDINGS: A STATELY CLASSICAL HOUSE IN A 'LANDSCAPE' SETTING

abundant on record. Over England as a whole, the yield of wheat passed 34 bushels to the acre; on favoured land it was over 50 bushels; stock-breeders and engineers could not satisfy the world's demand for English cattle and agricultural machinery. The railway net was practically complete, and it had covered the country with another net of hospitality, visits, and correspondence. If we set aside the definitely industrial areas, England was still a land of villages and little towns, over which the landed interest was dominant. The Reform Act had not seriously impaired its ascendancy; Free Trade had not diminished its wealth. High farming was the order of the day, and the results were visible in the growing rent-roll. The land was coining money, and the money flowed out, through the local bank to the London bank, from the London bank to the bill-broker, to finance the manufacturer, the shipper, and the merchant.

The development of communications, in which Dr. Arnold saw the end of feudalism, did in fact raise the country house to its final and brief splendour. By one of those unexpected turns which constantly meet us in history, it elevated the great house at the expense of the lesser houses. The squire's consequence diminished in the eyes of his neighbours, who could now go to London and there see for themselves with what grandeur Bowood and Woburn took the town; who could read for themselves of the fairy splendours of the Eglinton Tournament and the Chatsworth conservatories; who could visit a dozen palaces in a holiday tour, and study, as their taste preferred, Lord Darlington's model farm at Staindrop, the statuary of Ince Blundell, the pictures of Drayton, or the Duke of Bedford's cottages. Foreigners were dazed and the natives were dazzled, less by the accumulation than by the diffusion of wealth, of wealth which, whether it was drawn from trade or manufacture, from the East Indies or the West, could only display its full magnificence when it had been returned to the land. But apart altogether from those aspects of it which are preserved to us in Turner's 'Drawing Room at Petworth', or in those not less gorgeous descriptions, written half in mockery, half in adoration, with which the intellectual comedy of Disraeli's novels is diversified, this phase in the history of the country house had more sober and lasting consequences. Our public administration, even as we see it to-day, is in no small degree modelled on the administration of a great estate in the days when, in the nature of things, Cabinet Ministers belonged to the class of great landed proprietors, and were familiar, therefore, with the organisation and control of a large and highly specialised staff.

The social brilliancy and the political authority of the country house were the flower of its economic solidity, a solidity won by two generations of vigorous, scientific, often ruthless improvement, but precariously poised on the balance of home-grown and foreign-grown wheat. The tendency, visible from a very early date in our history, towards the aggregation of holdings was now working at full power, and the Continental visitor was at once impressed with the perfection of English farming and the exorbitant size of English estates. Many English observers contemplated the process with misgiving. Socially, the spectacle of a class almost inaccessibly rich and splendid was harmful, they thought, to the independence and culture of the people as a whole. Economically, the restraints on the sale of land, the law which gave the apparent owner only a life-interest in his property and transmitted it intact to one son, hampered improvement and checked the inflow of new brains and new money on to the land. By 1865 political speculators were very busy with the future, with the abolition of entail, the reconstitution of the peasant-holder or the owner-occupier as a class, the construction of agricultural co-operative societies. They need not have troubled. Nature has her own way of dealing with institutions which do not fit their age.

An observer in another planet might have remarked in the seventies a new phenomenon on the surface of the earth. Except in England, the gold was increasing against the green. He would rightly have inferred that a change of cultivation was in progress. He could not have known that he was watching the end of a social order.

> The cuckoo of a joyless June
> Is calling through the dark. . . .

The disastrous summer of that year 1879 was the beginning of a time of calamity which stretched to 1894, the driest summer within memory. The grazing counties came through with heavy but not fatal loss. The corn counties were stricken. There was a saying that with wheat at 50s. farming began to pay after 28 bushels had been got from the acre. After 1877 it never touched 50s. again, and the harvest of 1879 did not reach 16 bushels. In 1884 the price dipped below 40s.; in 1894 wheat was at 22s.; and indeed the harvest of that year of panic sold at 19s.; one German visitor wrote that soon not a wall or a tree would be seen for miles in England, and the whole rotten fabric would collapse in ruins. Another, better equipped and more sympathetic, laid his finger on the worst symptom of desolation. 'All over Norfolk,' he wrote, 'the Halls are shut up.' 'Take it away,' the last Doge of Venice said, as he handed the Ducal cap to his attendant, 'I shall not want it again.'

The magnitude and finality of the disaster to the landed interest was indeed masked by the fact that the surplus profit of the land had long been stored away in urban property, in bank stock and Consols, in commercial investments at home and abroad. The ancient distinction of land and money was passing away; and, thanks to the development of the limited-liability company, the landlord was able to remit his rents and maintain his mansion out of his earnings as a brewer, a banker, a tea merchant, a proprietor of railways in France and docks in America. The difference between those who stayed at home and those who went to London had reasserted itself in a new shape, in the difference between those who had something to draw upon, and those who had not. Thus, though the loss of annual and capital value in the years of depression was enormous, the fabric did not collapse so rapidly as the German visitor anticipated. The plutocracy was ready enough

64 PETWORTH HOUSE, SUSSEX: THE GREAT PARK

65 ASHRIDGE, HERTFORDSHIRE: THE GREAT LIME AVENUE

to take over the deserted halls, and the surviving aristocracy was itself plutocratic. Gradually the land righted itself, with milk and meat and vegetables in place of wheat; to a careless observer in 1900, looking, for example, to the great houses which were rising under the hands of Philip Webb and Norman Shaw, the landed interest might have seemed as solidly established as in 1850. Actually its roots had been cut. *Tolé questo: no la dopero piu.*

Looking at the matter in historic perspective, we may say that the hereditary landed interest ceased to be indispensable when the nation had created other and more effective organs of government and administration, culture and order, benevolence and science, in the rural regions. Ceasing to be indispensable, it had either to earn a new standing for itself or to disappear, and the process of extinction, deliberately expedited by Liberal finance, has in our time been further accelerated by the unforeseen and unprecedented burden of war taxation. In these circumstances the natural destiny of the great house which cannot support itself on its revenues is to be converted to public use, as a county building like Trentham, a school like Stowe or Weston Birt, a country club or a residential hotel. Other purposes can doubtless be contrived. Colleges at Oxford and Cambridge used to have Pest Houses, to which their members could retire in time of plague. Westminster School had one at Chiswick. Why should they not acquire country houses, for reading parties in the vacation? When the house is in itself and its surroundings a work of art, when it harbours a famous collection of pictures, books, tapestries, and furniture, then, as Lord Lothian has suggested, the owner might fairly ask that in return for admitting the public to enjoy its treasures, and keeping the house and estate in good condition, he should receive special consideration in the matter of estate duties. The family, in fact, would become hereditary custodians of a national monument; their taxation would be so adjusted that they might remain hereditary: if after all they were obliged to sell, the estate would pass under the same easements and advantages.

On the other hand, the smaller houses, which are less costly to maintain, will, with the development of communications, become more and more suburban. Already the Londoner can be in the Chilterns or the Kentish Weald in less time than it took Mr. Grote or Mr. Angerstein to reach his Blackheath villa. The inducements which in former ages drew rich townsmen into the country—a safe return on their investment, consideration, authority, gentility, rank—are ceasing to operate. The inducement, already visible in Defoe's account, to treat the country as a prolonged week-end grows greater. The grand jury has gone; the prospect of becoming a justice of the peace no longer figures in the advertisements of house-agents; as a local administrator the country gentleman's chief function is to back the intelligence of his experts against the penuriousness of his ratepayers, the Medical Officer against the local builder, the Director of Education against the farmer; to be urgent with town-planning, to protect what is left to be protected against the ribbon and the pylon, to lead in the advance towards better standards of building and greater care for the surviving amenities of the country. Taken together, they are not unimportant duties, and they are not unrewarded. What more is left for him to do seems to depend entirely on that incalculable element, our agricultural future. It is better not to speculate, but Clio always has a trick or two up her sleeve, and who can say that we shall not some day see Edward of Sarum back in his excellent house, under his old titles of Shire Reeve and Vice-Comes, new-translated, as District Bailiff and Deputy Director of the County Plan?

R. H. Mottram

THE COUNTRY TOWN

THE very name of the Country Town is a paradox. The words are a contradiction in terms, an attempt to unite two irreconcilables. To say that is to say that we are considering something supremely English in the widest sense of the word, which is larger than the seemingly more comprehensive term British.

The country town can be seen to its best advantage wherever that particular culture, or the lack of it, either unconscious feeling for a certain way of life, or deliberate preference for practice rather than theory, has grown up and expressed itself in that most fluid, least topical of all tongues, the English language. Its home is mainly along the coast of the Channel and North Sea, and it might not be difficult to find reasons for that if we did not distrust any argument founded on climate and situation, to which man has ever risen superior.

Let us be content to look for our typical country

66 NORWICH: THE SATURDAY MARKET BENEATH THE CHURCH OF
ST. PETER MANCROFT

67 ODIHAM HAMPSHIRE: A CORNER BY THE CHURCHYARD

town in England, and if not altogether in the southern and eastern portions of it, at least not in the remoter northern and western fringe. There is nothing in the country town of Celtic Twilight or Celtic fairyland, nor of that savage nobility that redeems and makes uncomfortable the small towns of Ireland and the Highlands. We need not, therefore, be accused of any narrow patriotism if we find our example of the country town at home. It clearly must not be large or specialised. We cannot fix a limit to its size, but the great port, or the busy, clanging, bustling hive of some particular industry, sets a limit to our search in another dimension. A crowded quay, a large factory, a university, a coal-mine, any pretension to a metropolitan influence takes us away from our subject. There is nothing in our country town comparable to the charming (that is beautiful and delectable) provincial town of France. There is no word in the English language to translate the French one '*province*'. It means exactly a town away from but governed by Paris, in a way our country town never is by London. The towns of Holland come near it, but they are too famous and too few. You cannot be sufficiently anonymous in those small places that have led the world, contain some of its greatest paintings, most renowned buildings, and highest tragedies of history. Nor need we be concerned with the offspring of the country town, true to type, which exists in North America. It is not old enough.

Now, therefore, having set such limits to our subject, having politely bowed and by-your-leaved ourselves space in which to consider, we may confess that we have, all the time, had in our minds the most perfect example of all country towns, Slowdon-in-the-Soke. Torture would not drag from us its geographical situation, for out of the forty-four counties of England we love precisely forty-four. But Slowdon will stand for something to be found in all of them. Slowdon possesses exactly those qualities which we have found lacking in the large, more important, more famous human congeries. They have their special reasons. They are too plainly connected with some great trade, administration, or faculty. Slowdon is not. It stands where it does by accident, and has been perpetuated by habit, and, above all, convenience; that is why it is the most comfortable place in the world. Violence has long deserted it, the stresses of the nineteenth century have passed it by. The febrile activities of the twentieth century have rendered it at once more accessible and more desirable. We will find out why.

For Slowdon does not advertise itself, and we who have discovered it are not going to tell all our friends exactly where it is. We do not desire to see its street congested with motors, lined with cafés, and diversified with dance-halls and cinemas. One of each is enough. Let those amenities cluster where life is so exacting that people need distraction, means of getting away from life in mind and body in order to endure it. Slowdon has, fortunately, no guide-book. Or, at least, none for a hundred years. At its stationer's we did find a little leather-covered volume, neatly bound and illustrated with beautiful plates, from engravings on steel. Its title-page, which faced one showing the abbey 'restored', says the text, 'to its pristine respectability by the munificence of Armine Bone, Esquire, Lord of the Manor', bears this informative inscription:

'A concise guide to the Beauties and Antiquities of Slowdon-in-the-Soke by Ph. Slapworthy, M.A.'

The preface to this work states that the intention of the author has been to present, for the information of the stranger, such of the *leading features* and *general views* as may be deemed interesting, in anticipation of the influx of visitors expected at the meeting of the Scientific Society.

'If it has no other merit' (Mr. Slapworthy continues, prefacing his Guide), 'it has at least that of aiming at a candid and impartial exposition of the subjects treated, and of forming an adequate reference to the several objects which chiefly merit the attention of a stranger, during a limited stay in the district.'

Mr. Slapworthy is altogether too modest. The fact is that he leads us straight to the first thing that we want to know. He states:

'A rapid glance at the history of Slowdon presents these marked and peculiar characteristics: War, Religion, Commerce.'

There we have it. We know why Bombay and Montreal and Melbourne stand where they do. But as for Slowdon, it stands where it does because a Roman military commander, sick of having his supplies cut off and his men ambushed, built a fort on the slight rise that dominates the shallow valley, then so intractable and wild, now so fertile and domesticated. The name Slowdon means nothing but the untilled mound, the lump of poor soil in which primeval forest grew thinner than elsewhere. Slowdon was just that, and happened to be about half-way, and in a mathematically straight line, between two Roman camps. That is how Slowdon came into being. As Mr. Slapworthy goes on to tell you, some years before he wrote—about A.D. 1800 by the imprint—the sexton who used to dig the graves in the wide graveyard of the Abbey Church dug up various objects—brooches, pins, small images, knife-handles— which, so Mr. Slapworthy declares, proved conclusively in the opinion of the wiseacres of that day, that the church itself stands on the site of a small temple to the god of the River Slowly, that winds through the fields below the town. The Christian church stood on pagan foundations in fact, a parable which would have shocked Mr. Slapworthy had it not been, fortunately, beyond his perception. What else the sexton of that day and of centuries before, right up to 1847 and the making of a new cemetery outside the town, may have dug up, of gold or silver, and disposed of for such a price as would purchase a gallon of beer, no one will now ever know.

Romans came and Romans went, but there remained the '-don' of Slowdon, the mound in the valley, and to-day the summit of this forms the market-place, the

68 BEDFORD: THE GEORGIAN BRIDGE OVER THE OUSE

69 CIRENCESTER, GLOUCESTERSHIRE: THE MARKET-PLACE, GUILDHALL, AND CHURCH

central open space of the town where roads meet, and is still, after all these centuries, called the 'Hill'. Below it, where the Romans made their little temple, there may have lingered some wooden shrine then or subsequently Christian. But, as Mr. Slapworthy has pointed out, the first reason for the place was War and the second Religion, and we must keep to this order.

To-day you will approach Slowdon by road, for it is essential to the character of the place that it missed the worst vicissitudes of the nineteenth century. Coal was never discovered near it, nor would its stream ever bear the burden of great ships, nor did its climate or its situation ever invite cotton or woollen manufacture, save such domestic weaving as may have been done for its own clothing. Thus it never became involved in the anxious and tragic history of transport trade. It even scouted the railway for a decade longer than larger towns, under the redoubtable lead of its great landowner of the family of Strongboys, who, as late as the year in which Mr. Slapworthy wrote, was still in a state of being loudly damned if he'd have smutty mechanic fellows grinning over his fences. That is why you approach the place from a better standpoint to-day than anyone has for a hundred years. For the railway is three-quarters of a mile away across the marshes, never seems to belong to the town, never did any great business, and now does less. And however lamentable this may be from some points of view it is due to these facts—climate, situation, and landowner—that Slowdon remains to-day literally our Country Town, not only a town in the country, but one into which the country comes invading even to its centre, as we shall see, as, averting our eyes from a few twentieth-century bungalows and Victorian villas, we change gear to engage in the ascent that leads us up to the 'Hill' in its centre.

Here we see the country town in detail. North of the Trent it may be largely built of solid blocks of stone. It will be grimmer, necessarily, for all around it on the green hill-tops hang the low clouds, and walls must be thick and roofs steep and solid to keep out all that ever-impending rain. Between the Thames and the Severn it will be built of a different and possibly more beautiful stone, and the gentler landscape, heavily wooded, or broken into gay squares of orchard, will show that suaver beauty which is perhaps the most English of all. Over most of the south and east, and most of all in the rich Thames Valley, it will be of rosy brick, with pantiles to match. Again, wherever the ancient forest lingered the longest, it may be of black timber with plaster worked into various patterns, and this may be handsomest of all in Essex or Cheshire. Occasionally, in East Anglia, there will be the wonderful translucent black flint, in Devon, granite again. They all have their beauty, and we will not be so peevish as to pick and choose among them, only allowing every man properly to prefer that in the shadow of which he grew up.

The reason for this huddle of old house-fronts, this furrowing of old roofs along the narrow streets that lead to the Hill, is War, Mr. Slapworthy will tell us, and we might well be astonished, did we not realise that he wrote these words in an ultra-safe island in a romantic age. It was war, if you like, which caused this agglomeration, but it was war long ago. We shall soon see, if we dive in between the massive gate-posts or under the low-browed entry that gives access to the yard of the 'Strongboys Arms'. At the back of the yard a twenty-foot green bank is tipped with trees, and if we scramble up among them we shall find ourselves on a grassy mound, whose queerly undulating surface is explained. Here stood the castle of the Strongboys, to whom the manor was given by Norman William. And, oddly enough, no sooner was that stronger and more intelligent pirate established firmly in his castle over the various other kinds of pirates (those whom we call the Anglo-Saxon and those whom we call the Danish, but who were in fact, all of them, boatloads of land-greedy, booty-seeking men, who became gradually appeased by loot and Christianity) than that castle ceased to have any importance. It was never attacked after the wars of the unfilial Plantagenets, mouldered down to a ruin, was used as a quarry, finally as a playground for children, a meeting-place for lovers. Ironic fate for the great keep which, Mr. Slapworthy will tell you, stood here to intimidate the countryside. It intimidated all too successfully, so that it destroyed its *raison d'être*. To-day the Urban District Council has received a gift of the site from the philanthropist who purchased it from the remote descendants of that once much-feared lord, and will find work for the unemployed, laying out the space as a garden. As for that one remaining shard of masonry, the half of the cylinder of the gate-tower that was added before the Wars of the Roses, the Councillors will have its frost-worn edges cemented and will put up a neat tablet to say what it is, and that children must not climb it, in a style that Mr. Slapworthy would thoroughly approve. For this green hillock with its crumbling stones is what he meant by War.

Now let us see next where Religion has shed its influence on Slowdon. Here again it must have been a long while ago: the streets of the town are bereft of image and gowned figure like any other town. But we can descend by a cobbled way that leads down from the castle ruins, past the pig-pens of the fortnightly Sale, that fills what was once the forecourt of the stronghold, along the backs of a score of little gardens that show how thoroughly the country has permeated the town. Here is none of the melancholy inhumanity of the centre of a big town where no one lives. Slowdon's inhabitants still have their 'bit o' land' at their own back-door, their rows of vegetables, their flower-borders, their hen-coops and green-painted summer-houses next to their wicket-gates.

We come thus into the street called Watergate and see before us unmistakably a church of no small pretensions, although we may have some difficulty in making out at first what has been done to it. It seems oddly truncated, and its tower has somehow arrived at its eastern end, while the west front—a handsome one— seems too grandiose for the foreshortened building behind.

70 THAXTED: A VIEW DOWN THE MAIN STREET FROM THE GUILDHALL

But Mr. Slapworthy will put us right. This is the church which was restored to its 'pristine respectability'.

Now, if we make a circuit of the tumbled and slowly subsiding rows of graves, until we approach the wall that used to protect the precinct from the flooding of the river, we can turn back and see, with Mr. Slapworthy's help, what has happened. Here was the priory of the monks, and here was the scene of everlasting contention between townsfolk who wanted a parish church and regular ecclesiastics who wanted a holy fortress from which the world might be excluded. And much trouble did the two factions cause successive generations of Strongboys who had given the land, and had promised to their tenants one thing, and to those who were to devote their lives to praying for the souls of Strongboys quite another. Good relations with those who tilled his land and provided to an increasing degree his income, were necessary to any man, and not least to those of large ideas such as the Strongboys ever were. And good relations in another world, to which he might always incontinently be hurried, were equally important to members of a family who lived up to the Strongboys' device of 'Strike first'.

The Strongboys compromised, as well they might in such a fix, and allowed the use of the nave to the parish and the chancel to the monks. Not that that arrangement stopped the broils which proceeded, even to the shedding of blood, the placing of the town under an interdict, and might be going on still had not there occurred the changes we know as the Reformation. The priory, spoken of by

Mr. Slapworthy and all his generation as the 'Abbey' was dissolved, its riches inventorised, its property sold, its images and furniture dismantled. The chancel was shorn off, but the nave, being the parish church, remained, and remains to this day, with a west front fit for a building twice the size, and far higher in consideration, and what had been the central tower now left at the east end of the surviving edifice. The great arch where the chancel should have continued was bricked up, solemn horse-box pews and a soberly furnished altar served the parish for several centuries more, until, in Mr. Slapworthy's day, a Strongboys of tender conscience and susceptibility cleaned up the wasted ruins of the outbuildings, repaired the tower, and gave the splendid reredos in the style of Viollet-le-duc, which we shall see if we step inside. Yes, you can soon tell. Something settled, something very old and sure of itself, inhabits this house of God that was first built with great solid piers and round-topped arches, and had that lighter clerestory added along with so many other details.

Now the whole has settled down, and you know you are in a country town. Here is no concession to the last two centuries and a half, very little to the two before that. Oliver Cromwell's adherents smashed the heads off those carved figures and whitewashed over those paintings. The headless figures remain to shame them, the whitewash has been flaked off carefully and the paintings treated so that you can see the familiar imagery of an earlier age, the Virgin and the Devil, St. Christopher of course, and possibly one of the first Strongboys giving the abbey (a little model, it may be, rests, very faded and indistinct, in the palm of his outstretched hand) to a figure which must be that of the prior, but perhaps the townsfolk scratched out his face in anger before ever Cromwell laid a ban on all such things.

We must be careful how we walk as we admire the somewhat florid pseudo-medieval reredos of a century ago. For the floor beneath our feet is paved, not with good intentions, but with lengthy justifications of all the more respectable dead who were found a place to lie, here in the holy fabric, while poorer Christians went to heap up the level of the graveyard outside, that stands some feet above the flagged passage, which certainly has not sunk. Here they are; 'Armigers' they liked to be styled if possible, and to have a coat of arms graven on their resting-place. Other generations specialised in the skull and crossbones and apt rhymes. Along the walls, too, and between the pillars of the arcade, are even more splendid tombs, where Crusaders recline, legs crossed, beside their wives. And here, in contrast, are the Elizabethans, bald and bearded, in trunk hose and doublet, opposite wives in cap and gown, with rows and rows of little boys and girls kneeling behind the parent of appropriate sex, testifying to their fertility and good family manners. Surely if age and use and wont and good order, and a quiet certainty about God and His personal jurisdiction over each one of us, make a place holy, then this is abundantly consecrated, even without those curious old crosses painted in circles on its walls.

Perhaps Mr. Slapworthy is right. If by War he meant

the protection, often oppressive enough, no doubt, of a strong castle, then it may have been War that fostered the growth of some sort of market, some sort of exchange of goods in the open space under the castle walls, where to-day the pig sale takes place on the Hill. Such an exchange was the beginning of civilisation, and it never occurred to Mr. Slapworthy that in fostering the market beneath its walls the castle was destroying itself.

Next he put Religion, and by Religion he meant this ancient, half-demolished place of sculptured stone and unconscious habit of phrases almost as chiselled and durable as the stones among which they have been repeated century after century. Mr. Slapworthy was really much more shrewd than he knew. Thirdly he put Commerce, little knowing what that word would come to mean during the hundred years after which he wrote, or what vicissitudes the thing he meant was to pass through, or what changes it was to bring about.

To see what he meant we must turn up the relatively steep Abbeygate, that leads up back to the Hill. All along the way we shall see what he, and indeed Slowdon generally, has always conceived to be commerce, a row of little shops whose owners lived over them, and sometimes still so live in Slowdon, though now they no longer make what they sell, as he supposed they always would. His mind was full of those images perpetuated on the cards with which the game of Happy Families was and still is played. He thought of Commerce, of the property of Slowdon, even of the world, in terms of Mr. Rolls

72 MARLBOROUGH, WILTSHIRE: THE BROADEST HIGH STREET IN ENGLAND

72 A STREET MARKET UNDER THE CASTLE WALLS, CONWAY

the Baker, Mr. Chips the Carpenter. He even had some
conception of public service as Mr. Atkins the Soldier
and Mr. Jack Tar the Sailor, Mr. Hose the Fireman,
and Mr. Bobby the Policeman, although this latter was
very new to Slowdon. He understood the professional
services of Mr. Pills the Doctor and Mr. Silence the
Usher.

But of mass-production he had no idea, and of mass-
distribution even less. Men worked; women, technically,
did not. They minded the house. That they ever did
anything else, Mr. Slapworthy ignored. And in Slowdon
he was justified in ignoring their other activities as he
was justified in ignoring overseas trade. Neither the
labour of women nor the remoter consequences of
Commerce made themselves felt in Slowdon, and do
not make much difference to-day. The great changes he
would see, could he mount Abbeygate with us on a fine
May morning, would be the advertisements of bananas,
chocolate, and cigarettes plastered over all the walls,
and packets and bunches filling so many windows, and
the motor-traffic in the streets with its inevitable petrol
stations, its characteristic smell, its nervous pace and
size. Abbeygate would have seemed to him an odd
place, with not merely no horse in sight but no patch
of horse-droppings anywhere, no smell or sound of
horse at all.

For Slowdon belongs to an older, pre-Victorian,
almost pre-Elizabethan England. It was, and largely
still is, a town of the old self-contained island that cared
nothing for Montreal, and was not affected in its politics

by Bombay. Europe even was a long way off, and its older inhabitants still speak of its younger ones as having 'gone foreign' when they go to London.

Here is the smithy, but it does not sound to the roaring of the bellows, the smiting of iron, the fidgeting of horses, nor does it smell of soot and scorched hoof as it once did. The smith can buy all the horse-shoes he is ever likely to need, and more, ready-made in sizes so graded that it is not worth while for him to hammer out his own. He has turned his attention to repairs to motor-vehicles, more especially delivery vans, and is adjusting himself to the change more rapidly than most of Slowdon. After all, he always worked in metal and was always concerned with the way people 'got about', as he would have put it. We call it transport to-day. The change is far greater as we approach the Hill, and come to the larger, more solidly built houses. Here is the chemist, nowadays almost entirely concerned with selling proprietary brands. He would do badly indeed if the new craze for health had not allowed him to let his ground-floor parlour to the dentist who visits once a week and caused him to become the local depot for the Red Cross. Gone from his window are the great carboys of green and red. And he is no longer consulted as he once was, on all sorts of subjects, from home-made fertilisers to astronomy. But whose fault is it? His own father's, who first bought a microscope and helped to found the Scientific and Philosophical Society that used to have its rooms next to the bank, where the great cinema is now. That was the circle in which men first began to ask

questions and to probe into reasons, that was the atmosphere, one of intelligence and humane curiosity, in which
began the process that has left Mr. Slapworthy's Slowdon
almost a museum-piece, a scarcely moving centre around
which a wider and wider and wider circle of human
existence revolves with ever-increasing speed. Let us go
on and see what changes have been wrought, but first
let us glance at the general layout of the Hill. It slopes
away a little southward from the castle site, and the
'Strongboys Arms' at the upper end probably marks the
barbican or other outwork, before which tenants bringing supplies to the fortress parked such beasts of burden
or even rough means of conveyance as they may have
possessed. As feudal rights and warlike necessity declined into ordinary buying and selling, the meeting-
place did not change; it was too firmly established.
Buildings had grown up along Abbeygate. Naturally
the other main track, round the hill and along the ridge
above the valley, intersected the downhill road that
crossed the river by the Prior's Bridge. As the lord of
the manor became increasingly an absentee, crusading
in Palestine or pushing his fortunes at Court, the more
and more widely enfranchised tenants held some sort of
moot or committee, and governed themselves as much
as he and the abbot would let them—not much at first
no doubt, but more as time went on. Like all other such
bodies, they developed a strong dislike to paying taxes,
and both the lord of the manor and the abbot found
that claims they based on ancient usage were constantly
being denied by a group of stubborn shopkeepers who

based their denials upon a growing list of charters obtained by judiciously lending money to the King. And some say that they were greatly helped to this course of action by one Simon whose house stood on a spot where there are still great groined cellars communicating, it is believed, with the castle. Of course the Jews were banished in A.D. 1290 but there is some reason to think that he, whose messuage stood on the spot that had belonged to 'Judeus Dives' the Goldsmith, may have been one of them, too useful, too intelligent to be spared, protected by the lord of the manor, perhaps, until he saw that even higher protection was necessary. However this may be, we know for certain that under Henry VII the Strongboys were shorn of most of their power; while under Henry VIII came that even more drastic assertion of royal will by which the prior was abolished, and the nave of the Abbey Church only survived for parish use. It must have been an age of profiteers made quickly rich. Land was the best understood, most generally desired form of wealth, and how much land came into the vigorous, grasping hands of men of humble origin who had never had much and felt they could never have enough! Now, at last, we come to something we can clearly see remaining for us. For although most of the houses round the Hill have had modern glazed shop-fronts put in, the upper storeys in at least a dozen cases show the spacious gables that were built under Elizabeth. When internal peace was assured, wealth became more and more diffused, and cattle and goods could be freely moved, and the strangers began to filter into Slowdon.

74 CHIPPING CAMPDEN, GLOUCESTERSHIRE: THE ALMSHOUSES
AND CHURCH TOWER

Then came Dutch-speaking weavers who taught the
at first reluctant and suspicious cloth-makers greater
skill and mystery in their craft. More cloth began to be
made in those upper rooms, where still the long, low
windows show how the looms increased, than could be
sold or worn in Slowdon, and it was sent overseas, as men
thought less and less about Europe and more about the
new sources of wealth on the other side of the world.

A Golden Age! Too golden and too brief. Its
excitement was too much for the lower-middle-class
heads of the men who were the masters of Slowdon,
instead of the great churchmen and nobles who were
gone. Money, some of them began to understand, was
better than land. They built themselves a Woolhall,
and many private dwellings. They built them too thickly
on the little patch of land around the Hill. And the next
thing they knew was that a great sickness had fallen upon
many, and the scenes of panic and bewilderment that
supervened around that overcrowded market-place are
told in old black-lettered books in many a library for
those who want to catch the sense of how a Visitation of
God presented itself to the man of that day. For us,
casual visitors, out along Eastgate, where to-day the
'buses change gear to climb the short ascent of the Hill,
there is still a field on which no one has ever built and
which now, happily enough, has become the recreation ground of the town. But those who like to pore
over old maps will find it marked plainly enough as 'pest
houses', and there the rotting corpses were hurriedly
bundled into long trenches, and sprinkled with lime and

covered up. And how long and how dire might have been the epidemic, and if it would have left much of Slowdon for us to visit, none can say, for it carried its own cure with it, in the infinite irony of Providence. In one of those terrifying summers of heat and drought, when the sickness raged, intermittent but never done with, the Woolhall caught fire. The Hill is nearly a quarter of a mile from the river, and we can easily imagine the line of frantic men passing wooden buckets from hand to hand, spilling half the water and never getting enough to the timber-and-thatch erection where so many hard bargains had been struck. It perished, and with it went all that eastern side of the buildings round the Hill. With it also went the sickness, either because the worst centre of perpetual infection lay somewhere around that spot, perhaps in the rat-infested yard where the dyestuffs, madder, and what-not were kept; or perhaps simply because it had worn out its virulence. And with it also went the cloth trade. But there again, who shall now say that the disturbance and loss of a great fire, or the gradual decline in personnel and in security of trading resulting from the sickness, caused the trade to go? Or would it have gone anyhow to the larger towns, the bigger markets, the places situated on wider rivers that would take a heavier type of barge for transport?

Certain, however, it is that the site long lay vacant, until, under James, there came a great revising and renewing of charters by the autocratic decree of that pedantic moraliser. And the upshot was that fine court-house that stands there to-day, so light and elegant with its tall windows of leaded glazing, its pillar steps and balustrade portico, hipped roof and clock-embossed pediment. The style varies, naturally, from Lauder to Stockton-on-Tees, from Bury St. Edmunds to Abingdon, but the intention is the same.

Little did James intend that it should be the meeting-place of the committee that declared against his successor in the Parliamentary Wars. The Hill resounded with the clank of pikemen exercising, the stamping of farm-horses brought in to carry hard-headed and hard-fisted men to battle, partly because they would not pay taxes, and partly because some at least felt that it was impossible to say what chance might not be turned to good account.

A second time war passed Slowdon by. There is nothing to be seen of the passions and defiances of those days but the splintered heads of the saints on the porch of the church. Mr. Slapworthy had his order of progress slightly wrong. War and Commerce had done with Slowdon, which, when a King had come again and gone, and yet another King reigned in his stead, reverted more and more to what it had once been: the handiest place for twenty miles to which the farmer could drive his cattle, buy a young horse, have his harness mended, and now even order a new wagon to be built.

But Religion had not done with Slowdon. The men of the place were all aggressively independent and jealous of anyone who got the better of them. Some were poor, some were violent, authority was weak and slow to move. With no great lord, spiritual or temporal over them, whom should they trust?

In one of the back lanes left between the more substantial houses lived Bone the Quaker. Who was he? A man of humble origin and rather poor physique, he had added to these disadvantages an odd, despised, and, at first, persecuted form of religious belief. He was punished for holding it, and when a none too strong and therefore tolerant government gave its protecting licence he still was laughed at and ill-treated. But the laughter died out and the ill-treatment ceased because it was evident that Bone's queer religion did make some difference to his daily life. He scorned all the powers and factions in the country—military force, wealth, and pleasure—but he was an astonishingly thorough and honest workman at his trade. Apparently his odd religion made him so. For the first time since the monks had been driven out two hundred years before, men saw religion influencing a man's daily life; his speech was full of it, it entered into all his dealings, it enabled him to bear threats and unpopularity, to scorn trickery, and to avoid malice. And, as the years went by, it became obvious that he was prospering. He bought his own house and workshop, he became better, if still soberly, dressed, he had money—he even gave it away. He was difficult to talk to, had an odd phraseology of his own, but he was straightforward. The words he said meant exactly what they stood for, once they were familiar. The times were still rough and uncertain. If a house caught fire it usually burnt to the ground. Robbery was frequent and often undetected and unpunished. The very allegiance of men to the new Royal Family, the fate

76 SALISBURY: THE COLLEGE OF MATRONS AND THE
CATHEDRAL SPIRE

of England among the nations of the world, the safety of goods and travellers on the road, a hundred yards outside the town, were often all uncertain. But Bone seemed to lead a charmed life. Disaster seldom overtook him, his house and goods, his family, and the growing circle of Friends, as they called themselves, who gathered round him, were like him, and were even now beginning to build themselves the oddest and plainest of little meeting-houses, in which, on Sunday mornings, they would sit with no altar, no outward sign, nothing on its bare walls, in silence so complete that it was intimidating. And in that silence one of them would quietly arise and speak, as if holding a private conversation with God. Bone grew older, more placid, more and more prosperous. His son grew to manhood beside him, a big burly fellow, twice the man his father had ever been, having never known the hardships, the poor health, the contempt his father had once endured. Far from it: men sought out young Bone, asked him to take care of their spare cash, asked him to send money for them if they had need to transact business far away. When the wine-merchant and brewer with the big new house that can still be seen over there on the west of the Hill drank and speculated himself into insolvency, young Bone bought the house and business, including the maltings down by the river. He doubled the size of the old office, and on one side affixed a brass plate stating that it was a Bank. He printed and issued notes, and people took them readily instead of coin. Why not? The notes said that Bone 'promised to pay the bearer'. It was certain that he could pay and equally certain that he would. The bank prospered. It became the dominating feature of the Hill. More gigs and wagons and saddle-horses stood before it on Sale days than before any other two houses in the town. And the bank began to set a standard of quality as well as quantity.

Old Bone died, and young Bone bought a farm. He farmed it as no land had been farmed before, and all the better farmers hastened to imitate him. They grew better crops, better-fed stock. The Sale increased. Bone bought the castle from the declining and impoverished Strongboys, and gave it to the town. It is the Sale-ground to-day.

Then on Sale days, when the 'Strongboys Arms' and all the lesser inns discharged their crowd of farmers and drovers, noisily full of Bone's Ale, it could be plainly seen that before and around the bank the crowd was soberer, more decorous, better dressed. The old days of drink and horses, and 'I-care-for-nobody, no-not-I', were becoming discredited because fewer and fewer people were content to face the natural corollary 'Nobody cares for me'. That accounts for the solider appearance of the western end of the Hill, for men began to build in brick with stone dressings instead of the timber which will warp and contract, not to say split and burn, while the old undressed stone buildings hold a mortal chill. And not only that, but there was also some attempt to regulate better the lives of the people. That meant not only Poor Law, and some attempt at paving, which is still visible in the back lanes, but the fine old Georgian wing of the infirmary, now the County Hospital behind the castle, was built then, and the great warehouse that the brewery now uses in Mill Lane was the Ragged School of that age.

As the eye travels along the southern façade, there at the corner of Abbeygate it may pause on the sign of the Waterloo Tavern. It is all that remains of a phase of Slowdon life that was significant enough while it lasted, with the constant trampling of marching men, and the call for facilities for feeding them, and the opportunity to supply them with beer that meant in those days almost the only alleviation of the lot that was hard, the only respite from a boredom that was nearly universal. It may not be fanciful to see something of the grim stresses of the times reflected in the architecture of the tavern, which, still solid, has none of the spaciousness and grace of the houses not far from it.

It was only a phase, though it was a long, no doubt to those who lived through it, apparently an interminable one. It left some terrible consequences in the shape of hectic trade booms and financial crises. Amid the reverberations of these we come back to Mr. Slapworthy, who was 'post-war' just as we are. After years of being taxed and frightened and bullied, peace came, and people in 1838 knew as little then as now what to do with it. Fortunately it left less trace, if anything, than the war of these days. Perhaps a few solid-looking villas called 'Orthes' or 'Douro Villa', in Strawberry Hill Gothic, survive in the road leading out into the country, to show where the profiteers of a century ago shook off the dust in which they had made their money and moved out, as they hoped, into gentility. This brings us back to Mr. Slapworthy. He wrote his Guide early in an age which was one of reform, of progress, of enlightenment. The new improved cottages that the descendants of Bone built on the land they had purchased from the even more descended Strongboys, and which we think so ugly, show something of the intention of the time. But Mr. Slapworthy and his Guide are the fine flower of it, and we want to reach back to him, and to picture him, the first person to regard his Slowdon self-consciously, to realise that it had a past, and to hope it might have a future. Let us therefore turn down Westgate, which soon brings us to the fine gate-posts, the spear-headed railings, the dark yews of the rectory. It must have been on the finer moonlit nights of autumn and winter that he would issue forth after tea, with his leather portfolio under his arm, to attend the meetings of the Slowdon Scientific and Philosophical Society. As he emerged from his gate, he would glance down the street, to see the weather-vane on the church tower gleam in the moonlight, as the rising wind hurried, piling clouds, across the night sky, and form his own conclusions based on experience and deduction, as to the probable course of the weather. Then he would turn up Westgate, unlighted, save where private bounty or public spirit chose to hang out a lamp. The windows were all shuttered, and the projecting door-steps protected by little railings. A few are left. He might meet the sexton going with his implements to dig a grave and speak benignly to the

78 SUMMER AFTERNOON AT BRIDGWATER, SOMERSET

79 REIGATE, SURREY: THE TOWN HALL

80 RYE, SUSSEX: MERMAID STREET

man, if sober, or severely to him if, as was likely, he were drunk. Emerging upon the Hill, he turns to see if the chemist is coming along from Abbeygate, or the doctor from his handsome house, the trees in the garden of which can be seen just beyond the court-house.

If he does not see them he turns in up the yard of the 'Strongboys Arms', passes the gust of noise and tobacco-smoke that eddies out from the bar, passes the bar-window of Mrs. Pardon's parlour, that enables her to look up and down the yard. Its blinds and curtains are drawn now and he goes farther, to the small side-door that opens under the vine that climbs all over the side of the house upon the little 'Snug' as it is called, where the Society still meets, though plans are on foot to take the house next the bank and open public rooms there.

The Snug is a panelled room, rather low, with a wide mantelpiece, above which, upon a baize-covered board, various items of interest to the coach-using public are set forth in printed bills. Above again is a picture of a race-horse. A bright fire burns below, and beside it the lawyer, Underwood, is talking to Bone, who, for all his money, still lives over the bank.

Mr. Slapworthy greets them, and they wait until the doctor and the chemist, and the agent for what remains of the Strongboys' estate, mostly mortgaged, have come in.

Mr. Slapworthy watches them as they order themselves a little refreshment, prior to the business of the evening. Bone drinks tea. Easily the wealthiest man there, he is most abstemious. The chemist is not so much abstemious as unable to appreciate flavours, which are, to him, the effect of alkalis and acids on the palate. The doctor, on the contrary, orders a bottle of port, and Mr. Slapworthy himself, a glass. The agent drinks rum shrub, and the lawyer brandy and water. When they are suited, the chemist and the agent light long churchwarden pipes.

Mr. Slapworthy unties his leather case, produces the plans they are to discuss for a great increase in the Society's activities, involving the purchase of a piece of land next the bank, which Bone will let them have on the most nominal terms, covered over and over again by his subscription. The lawyer will see to the settling of it on trustees, nominally those present, the agent will find a respectable builder, who is to submit plans for the erection of an Athenaeum and Institute, where there shall be a reading-room, a lecture-hall, and various other amenities. The chemist contends that the well of the Bank House contains iron solution, and wants to open a Pump Room and make the place a spa. But the lawyer is dubious, the doctor scornful. He is of the opposite school:

'Fresh air and more food, that's what people want—look at me. Always out in my gig, all weathers, go into the worst places, dank old houses where they starve themselves. Take a good breakfast before I go, bottle of port in the evening! See you all out!'

Bone does not contradict, but looks at him quizzically, as if remembering the fluctuations in his bank-balance, and only says:

'Wages must rise, cottages should be rebuilt. People should be taught to read. They'd look after their health then!'

The agent does not like this.

'Can't pay the labourer more than he's worth,' he declares, reflecting that Bone would like to take more money out of land and put it into trade.

The lawyer, however, does not back him up, as usual, but runs off at a tangent:

'It is true that many estates might still be improved. What the town wants is Industry!'

Mr. Slapworthy interposes gently, shepherding them back. As enlightened men they desire to exchange views, to exercise the mind, he suggests. As Christians they desire to raise the level of the lives of the less fortunate of the townspeople. Bickering a little, and each a little intent on his own point of view, they are persuaded to bend their attention to the matter in hand. They make such progress on this and subsequent nights that, before the young Queen comes to the throne, the Athenaeum and Institute is built, solid and four-square, with a pillared portico, and a little glazed lantern above its upstairs reading-room. Bone is the mainstay of the funds, the agent supervises the erection, the lawyer draws the deeds, the doctor presides urbanely, bowing to the gentry who meet in it in the morning, the chemist and Mr. Slapworthy give lectures and encourage the young men of the labouring classes in the evening, with such success, in their several ways, that, as the Guide proudly says, the Scientific Society elects to hold its meetings there in 1838.

Nearly a hundred years later we can follow the footsteps of Mr. Slapworthy and his fellow-members of the

Improvements Committee ('*Perseverendo*' was their motto)
better than those of almost any similar set of people of
the England of his day. Amid much that has changed
and that many of us feel to be crumbling, Mr. Slapworthy's
Slowdon has drawn itself together, concentrated its
slowly acquired and therefore solid strength. A few
more threats of aerial warfare, another currency crisis,
and Slowdon may emerge, as a place of refuge, one of
the few spots where people produce more of the necessities of life than they consume, and those in safety. It
is becoming daily more and more England, even when it
happens to be as far north as Haddington, as far west as
Helston, as remote as Beaumaris. It is actually strength-
ening its claim to be representative, which no great
cosmopolitan centre, no great port or nineteenth-century
industrial town, can challenge. The railway affected it
very little. The 'Strongboys Arms' felt it the most. The
decline of the coach, the linking up with great towns to
which money flowed and from which the new refine-
ments of life came, drained the traffic from the old inn
beneath the Castle Mound. But now that so much
traffic has come back on to the road the case is altered.
The luncheon menu hangs freshly written each day by
the old timbered entry, and the wide old yard, so long
deserted, is now a garage and petrol-station. Next to it,
the Athenaeum has become the Royal Cinema, it is true.
What would Mr. Slapworthy make of the enlightenment it sheds? Bone, however, would find its morals
unimpeachable. He no longer lives over the bank; his
very name has been swallowed up, with five-score others,

81 OLD HOUSES IN COLCHESTER, ESSEX

82 TUDOR HOUSES AT CORSHAM, WILTSHIRE

82   CAMBRIDGE: THE MARKET-PLACE AND GREAT ST. MARY'S

in a great combination stretching from Shanghai to Vancouver and down to Adelaide. The last of his name, however, bought and gave the castle which the Urban District Council have so tastefully laid out, while the farther part, where the old common meadow was, has now been properly accommodated with pens and sheds for the pig Sale, so that the square of the Hill is now a Car Park, and a stopping-place for buses. Here, too, the drinking-fountain of the R.S.P.C.A. is balanced by the War Memorial, and between these the chemist parades the Red Cross detachment on those occasions when we honour the King, or remember 1918.

The Waterloo Tavern has not held the popularity it recovered during war years. Bone's Brewery (long amalgamated with a great London one) brews as much beer as ever, but people no longer sit in the 'Waterloo' to consume it because they have nowhere else to go. The remains of the Library from the Athenaeum have been moved into the court-house; there is the cinema, but above all, there is the increasing comfort of their own firesides or back-gardens, especially since the doctor's successor, who is Medical Officer of Health, has had all the old insanitary rookeries pulled down and little crescents and quadrangles of new cottages built out half a mile along the main road. The little forest of wireless masts above the chimneys is another explanation, the frequency of newspaper shops another, while the expansion of old Miss Dumply's pastry-cook shop, that used to sell a few little tarts, into the Georgian Café, is a third, accounting sufficiently for the decline of the

'Waterloo'. The lawyer would be surprised to learn that the petty sessions have not had a case of drunkenness before the Bench for weeks, and that the magistrates' time is nearly entirely occupied with motoring and insurance offences.

Let us not leave Slowdon without passing down Abbeygate to glance at Mr. Slapworthy's church. Very astonishing is its present condition. For the morning congregation is not a third of what it once was, despite the closing of the meeting-house Bone used to attend and the decline in other dissenting places. The scandalous old graveyard is laid out as a pleasant garden, the fabric is well preserved, the decorations and furnishings, if a little 'high' for some persons' taste, are worthy and beautiful. An odd thing has happened to the Abbey Church, as it is still called with less reason than ever, something very English, which epitomises the general position of Slowdon better than any other building, and more clearly. The less people believe in that handsome, venerable, and sacred, if truncated, edifice, the more careful and respectful towards it they are. When it was literally their church and they spent at least some hours each Sunday in it, they allowed it to be dirty, distressingly plain, ill repaired, and locked for most of six days of the week. Now that they regard it as an interesting, moving, perhaps even inspiring survival, they will pay money and much attention to it. The change from a subjective, grudging possessiveness to an objective, aloof acceptance has been most marked. And herein lies perhaps the hope of the future, and Slowdon's contribution to the saving of the world. For what is true of the Abbey Church is true of Strongboys and their castle, of the prior, even of Mr. Slapworthy and Bone and his bank. Had all those persons and privileged positions, establishments and hierarchies remained powerful and integral as they once were, the forces of change and growth would long ago have been forced to accept the challenge and burst violently through them, obliterating Slowdon and all it contained. But this gentle relegation to the role of a dignified historic shell, within which new men, new thoughts, new life can find shelter, permits the face of the Past to be saved. The description of Slowdon as a country town may lose its half-tolerant note, and come to mean the only town that we can or desire to live in.

George A. Birmingham

THE
COUNTRY CHURCH

ONE day, while the war was in full course, I sat in
a little garden near Boulogne with two men, both
of them chaplains to the forces, as I was. We were tired,
profoundly bored, and not a little homesick. We talked,
as many men did in those days, of what we should like
to do and how we should like to live when the war was
over. My two friends had the same wish. They desired
nothing better than to settle down as parish priests in
some English village, a village with white cottages, many
trees, a gently wandering little river, and, above all, an
old church, venerable and grey.

It was a natural wish, for of all things on earth there
is nothing which makes so clear a promise of peace as
an English village such as my friends described, and
peace, the peace of long days of undisturbed monotony,
was what we all desired.

I, an Irishman and therefore a stranger, understood

84 BROMHAM, WILTSHIRE: THE PERPENDICULAR CHANCEL

85 STOURTON: A RICH LITTLE CHURCH OF THE WILTSHIRE DOWNLAND

their desire. I even shared it, though I had then no knowledge of English rural life, or even of English life at all except in great towns and cities. I had seen English villages, catching passing glimpses as I rushed from place to place in trains. Even those glimpses left me with a sense of curious intimacy between the churches and the villages they served. Sometimes I had gone wandering on a bicycle or on foot and seen more of these hamlets clustering round their churches. No other country has anything to show comparable to this. Our great cathedrals are matched, perhaps outshone, elsewhere. Parish churches in towns, equal to ours in stateliness and beauty, are to be found in many lands. But the English village church, with the nestling cottages and the manor-house, is unique. France, Germany, and Italy have nothing like it.

I understood that my companions in that French garden were looking for something more than peace when they craved to live in an English village with an old grey church. They wanted to get back to England itself, to that intimate soul of England which eludes us in the great cities, even in the quiet country towns, which we reach most easily and certainly in villages.

The village and the church belong to each other. It is not as if someone, some remote person or still remoter committee, had ever said, 'Here is a settlement of people. It is good for them to have a church. Let us build one for them.' This is what is happening to-day in mushroom garden cities and such places, whose people, overflowing from cities where they work, make play-grounds and sleeping-places in suburban districts. The Church, with laudable zeal, is doing its best to supply the spiritual needs of these camps. Our architects are designing churches which are both stately and beautiful, wisely eschewing facile imitations of the old, and building in the spirit of a new age. But one thing it is impossible for them to achieve: the sense of unity—the home-feeling —between the church and the houses round about it. Their churches may be beautiful, stately, convenient, even inspiring, to worshippers, but they remain things imposed from outside. This is inevitable, for there does not and cannot exist in these new settlements the community of life and interest which made the English village a sort of family home. The dwellers in suburbs and garden cities are people of widely different interests, united only by the accident of a common place of residence. Their church can be nothing but another public building erected, for a special purpose, in their midst. The true village church is something quite different. It is a natural part of a body with a life of its own, an expression of a unity of spirit. It is a home to which children gather from time to time feeling that it is theirs. It has not been imposed upon the village; but has grown out of it and with it. In a certain sense it may be said that it and the village are one.

If there is usually a marked outward and spiritual unity between the church and the cottages clustering around, what of the districts like Somerset and East Anglia, where the church is often of a size and magnificence to dwarf the humbler dwellings of man? Here the relationship is more of the nature of harmony in contrast; yet there is no disunity between church and village, even though the medieval wealth has long vanished, and the splendid building could accommodate several times over the shrunken farming population. In the glorious Perpendicular of Somerset or East Anglia we do not miss that connection with the people's life which is so outstanding when we look at the lowlier shrines of Sussex, where it almost seems as if the churches had grown with and out of the villages. But the greater churches have in some way accommodated themselves, as a great lady of very fine temper might find her home in a humble place and make her life one with that of simple people.

It is interesting, too, to note the way in which the builders of our village churches were influenced by their surroundings. Nothing is more striking than the harmony which exists between the church and the landscape of the district in which it has been placed. Take, for instance, the church of Blanchland, which serves a grey hard village set among barren Northumbrian hills. The church gives the impression of grim strength; there is little sweetness, small sign of graciousness about it. But there is strength. We feel that winter storms will sweep over it, piling the snow in drifts against its walls; but the church will stand firm as the bare hills around it. It is not a church to love tenderly, but a church to trust. No other kind of fabric could fittingly have been built in such a place. Or consider the little church which lies in its nook, almost under the shadow of St. Katharine's

Hall near Bath. Here is a building, simple yet of exquisite beauty, with terraced gardens leading to it, which has been well loved and is still loved, tenderly, as if it were a child, but a child with all the mystery of Bethlehem about it. Could the Blanchland Church have been built there, or it at Blanchland?

Or think of the fine parish church at Hartland, a building in which the grand medieval chancel screen survives. It is a solitary church, with no village nestling round it. It stands on a high plateau, not far from the cliffs which face the Atlantic storms and check the march of the Atlantic waves. How splendidly suitable to its surroundings is this unsheltered lonely church! Compare it with the little church at Dinder, standing among the trees in the park of a great house. It seems part of the appendage of the house and serves there a small community, whose lives in the past were linked in dependence with the life of the family who were owners, friends, patrons of land, village, and church. Here again there is a sense of fitness in the building itself. It could not be where Hartland Church is, or Hartland Church among its bee-haunted limes.

No more than vestiges survive of the earliest churches of all, and their origin is largely guesswork. But when we come to the great ages of church-building we are on surer ground. Who built and who planned our churches? These are the questions which we ask, happily not altogether without finding answers.

Towards the erection of our greater ecclesiastical buildings kings made gifts, truly royal in their munificence.

We have it on the authority of Wordsworth that such gifts were sometimes regarded as too generous. 'A royal saint' might be charged 'with vain expense', and that not only by the profane and secular-minded. St. Bernard, for instance, was no indiscriminate favourer of the Cluniac passion for great buildings. In their book on *The Medieval Mason* Professor Knoop and Mr. Jones refer us to several strictures on 'vain expense' made not by the secular-minded worldling, but by saints.

Noblemen, bishops, and monastic bodies were from time to time as generous as the kings in providing funds for the building of great and important churches. But we can hardly look to such sources for the provision of village churches. Now and then some lord of the manor, as in the fourteenth century Sir William Trussell at Shottesbrooke in Berkshire, might charge himself with the cost of building a village church. Now and then some monastic body, which had acquired for its own use the ecclesiastical revenues of a parish, was pricked in conscience and built or re-built a village fabric. But perhaps most commonly the funds and the labour were provided by the village itself, as may be seen in the fascinating story of the rebuilding of St. Petrock Bodmin in 1469–72, the largest church in Cornwall. Sometimes the gifts were entirely voluntary; sometimes at a later period money was raised by what we should now call a local rate; sometimes it was raised, as it is to-day for church purposes, by the sale of things which people more or less willingly bought. Ale was brewed and sold for the benefit of the church, and it is likely enough that the people bought that more readily than we now buy the pincushions and knitted jackets offered to us at charity bazaars. Nor need the use for church purposes of profit made from ale shock even those most devoted to what is called temperance when we consider that Dublin owes the restoration of its two cathedrals to a similar trade. St. Patrick's was restored by beer; Christ Church by whisky.

At certain times, the great periods of church-building, the people, and the villagers as much as any others, wanted churches, and by one means or another got them. The old buildings were too small for the use of a growing population, or they failed to satisfy the popular aesthetic instinct. Larger churches or more beautiful churches were desired. Or the spirit of rivalry arose. Another village, through some cause, had a larger and better church; why should 'our village' be left behind? This local emulation was especially marked in the South-west in regard to rood-screens. In 1446 the wardens of Yatton rode out to Easton-in-Gordano to inspect the rood-loft and investigate the cost. The work on their 'rodelofte' or 'Aler' went on until 1458, 'payenter' and 'ymage maker' playing their parts, but Crosse the carpenter did the main work. Once 2½d. was laid out for 'ale gevyn to Crosse to make him wel wellede', and as a final compliment he received a pair of gloves costing tenpence.

We must remember also that in the village the church was the only public building and therefore used for meetings on public business. As the village became more self-conscious and undertook the conduct of its own

86 WHITCHURCH, BUCKINGHAMSHIRE: THE APPROACH TO THE
CHURCHYARD

87 GODMANCHESTER, HUNTINGDONSHIRE:
A WELL-PROPORTIONED SPIRE

affairs, something like a parish hall became necessary, and the church served the purpose, if it were sufficiently large—served the purpose well if it were also impressive.

The motives for building were diverse and mixed, as all human motives are; but doubtless there was always present a sense that the building was done for God, to His greater glory. At all events it seems plain enough that the village churches were built in accordance with the will of the people themselves. The gifts of the great and mighty, of kings, noblemen, bishops and abbots, were but expressions of what was in all men's hearts. Can we wonder then at the intimate union which existed and still exists in villages between the church and the people?

Of the planning and designing of our village churches we know something, though not as much as we might wish. We have in some parts of the country magnificent village churches, but the names of few builders survive. The years following the Great Fire saw the rebuilding of many of the London city churches. The work is associated with the name of a great architect, Sir Christopher Wren, whose genius inspired all the work done then and there. The fifteenth century was a similar great period of church-building in Somerset, and we find in the splendid Perpendicular churches of the time, especially in their magnificent towers, the same evidence of unity of spirit. But we have no record of the name of any single man whose genius dominated the minds of his contemporaries.

Very often our village churches are closely knit with

the history of the great families which owned the surrounding land. There are monuments, proud altar tombs, recumbent figures of knights, and mural tablets, such as those of the Bedfords at Chenies and the Norfolks at Arundel. Sometimes these occupy places apart and are set in chapels reserved for such memorials. The chapels were built perhaps as chantries by pious lovers of the dead. They have long ceased to be used for their original purposes, but remain, mute witnesses to the former sway of prayers and masses. They are pages of English history written in imperishable stone, preserving great names and the memory of great deeds.

The village which the church serves has changed out of all recognition, changed in outward form, in spirit, and in the manner of men's lives. The church remains an unchanging witness to the faith which in great essentials changes not. But the church itself has developed, as the faith has, adapting itself to the spirit of each successive age. It is rare, though not impossible, to find a church which, architecturally, is just as its first builders left it, such as the little Heath Chapel remote in Salop. Occasionally the oldest church has totally disappeared, leaving no more perhaps than a font or a piscina to witness that it ever existed. Fifteenth-century builders. perhaps, have erected a wholly new building in their own manner, and after-generations have let it alone, neither building more nor pulling down. But for the most part this is not what happened. That distrust of drastic change, which is one of the characteristics of Englishmen, led our village church-builders to preserve the old where they could, throwing out an aisle sometimes to meet the needs of a growing population, or raising a clerestory, or adding a chapel for the use of a guild, or occasionally, as at Leigh-on-Mendip, for the special benefit of pilgrims on their way to or back from some famous shrine. The result is that many of our older churches are patchworks of various styles and witness to the changing needs of the generations which used them.

There were in medieval times no architects in the strictly modern sense of the word. There were masons and master-masons; under them, when the building was in progress, were unskilled labourers recruited locally. In the case of the greater village churches the masons of some guild were employed to plan and oversee the work, which was, to a large extent, done by men of the parish itself. These migratory bodies of masons were men of skill and experience. They had built elsewhere and in building had learned much, so that their work was in a continual state of development. They had a dominating conception of style, the style of their period, but they were always learning by actual experiment how best to realise the idea which somehow had come to possess their minds.

It is unnecessary here to trace the development of the different styles of architecture from Saxon to Norman, from Norman to Early English and from that on to the splendours of Perpendicular. The work has been done over and over again in learned and in popular books, and no one now who is interested in our English churches need lack a guide which will help him in his fascinating study. But it may be well to note—for this point deserves to be emphasised—how much the form of our village churches depended on the material easily obtainable. The transport of large masses of stone was very difficult and, where waterways were not available, enormously expensive. Great churches, built by wealthy communities or patrons, might be able to import stone from Caen. It was, as we know, so imported for use in the building of old St. Paul's, and later on in large quantities for Eton College. But it was plainly impossible for village builders to incur such expense; for their churches they necessarily depended on local material. Those fortunate enough to have good building stone near at hand, as in Lincoln and Somerset, built greatly, rejoicing in the erection of fine towers. In the case of one parish known to me, Mells in Somerset, the quarry from which the stone was hewed for the fifteenth-century church survives a few hundred yards from the building, and it is still possible to see half-hewn blocks of stone which for some reason were discarded by the builders. There the stone was of a very fine quality, not unlike the Doulting stone which is quarried to-day, though somewhat harder. With such a material at hand the builders could and did erect a fine church and a great tower. The same thing is true elsewhere. A man possessed of a geological map of England, marking the belt of oolitic limestone, might, without further knowledge, without visiting a single church, plot out the localities of the great church towers and spires, so intimate is the connection between the buildings and the accessibility of material.

88 CLARE, SUFFOLK: A FLINT CHURCH OF EAST ANGLIA

89 MORSTON CHURCH, NORFOLK, OVERLOOKING THE SALT MARSHES

90 MORWENSTOW, CORNWALL: THE CHURCH AND RECTORY

Elsewhere, in less fortunate districts, only inferior or less adaptable materials were available, and we have less grand, but not less gracious, village churches. Even very intractable materials like flint were used with skill and effect by village builders where no more 'workable' material was available. Wood, of course, was largely used in districts rich in trees but poor in minerals. The important thing to note is that in village churches, whatever may be the case in cathedrals and abbeys, the use of local material was universal. Men built as their material allowed them to build, thus establishing an intimacy between the village and its church which would perhaps have been impossible had the transport of material from a distance been cheap and easy.

Dr. Cox, in his deeply interesting volume *Church-warden's Accounts*, has cleared the reformers of the charge of having been the first to introduce pews into our churches. Pews existed and were appropriated to particular persons long before the Reformation, and if any blame attaches to anyone in the matter it ought to be laid on the shoulders of squires, patrons, and other people of importance in the parish, whether lay or clerical. It appears that this appropriation of seats was very early —as it still is—a fruitful subject of dispute. A fourteenth-century Bishop of Ely legislated on the subject, reserving the right to own pews to certain 'patrons of churches only', a curious disregard of St. James's precepts about church sittings. Pews and seats were even rented and purchased as early as the latter part of the fifteenth

century, and the money so made was part of the income
of the church and sometimes amounted to a considerable
sum. Our ancestors were, it appears, quite as widely
awake to the possibilities of this source of revenue
as their nineteenth-century successors in Kensington.
Among many instances seats were first let at St. Edmund's
Salisbury in 1477–8, and in the early sixteenth century
'the good wiefe of the blew bore' paid 4d. for her pew,
but next year for 'the good wyfes daughter' the rate
shot up to 20d. In 1623–4 the pews were numbered, and
by 1641–2 the receipts had risen to £13 9s. Similarly, at
St. Laurence Reading, Abbot Faringdon paid in 1501–2
'for his moder sete, iiijd', and in 1527 a Mr. Barton gave
'for a seate for his madens, viijd'. By 1607 no less than
293 seats were allotted throughout the church, at a
rental of £4 6s. 4d.

But the older churches were originally without pews.
It was my good fortune once to see a fifteenth-century
Perpendicular church from which the pews had been
removed for the purpose of renewal. There was no
doubt about the original intention of the builders.
The arcade of the nave gained enormously in dignity
and grace of proportion by the display of the lower parts
of the pillars, usually concealed by the pews built round
and against them. The pews by dwarfing the pillars
had injured the whole proportion of the building.

Most of our old village churches contained originally
no provision for the seating of worshippers except
narrow stone slabs, built either against a wall or round
the bases of the pillars. These were intended for infirm

persons—a possible origin of our saying, 'the weak to the wall' which has now come to have a totally different meaning. One result of this emptiness of the nave of the church was that it was much more suitable for secular use than any church is now. To the medieval mind there was little or no distinction between 'secular' and 'sacred'. This cleavage, which we call reverence, is a development of much later growth, a very gradual accretion which, however deep-seated and natural it may appear to us, has perhaps been not altogether free from artificiality in its results. Even in the seventeenth century the church discharged many functions now considered the province of the municipality. Dr. Coulton, than whom no one has fathomed more deeply the spirit of the Middle Ages, feels that to priest and people it was the most natural thing in the world to brew ale and sell it for the benefit of the church. The medieval English villager wanted to act plays in his church, to drink ale in it, even to dance in it, and the empty nave gave him his opportunity. He was often encouraged by his parish priest, who saw no harm in such practices. Bishops and saintly men protested, but for the most part protested without much effect. On this subject Mr. Powys has much to say which is interesting, and the curious reader should consult his *English Parish Church*. He attributes the final suppression of such practices to the joint efforts of Archbishop Laud and the Puritan party—a curious pair of allies in any religious work.

Yet, in spite of Laud and the Puritans, the church remained far down into the eighteenth century a centre of the village life. It ceased, indeed, to be a place of buying and selling. But it remained the home of associations and friendly societies (not unlike the medieval guilds) which used it freely on their high-days and holidays, marching to it with their emblems and away from it to their feasts. The churchwardens met there in vestries and there smoked their pipes (long clay pipes one hopes) while they discussed the imposition of a church rate, the minimum nourishment on which the life of a pauper could be sustained, and the terms of apprenticeship for orphans left to the care of the parish. It was there that they discussed the amount which should be paid for the slaughter of adders and polecats, or the smaller rewards of industrious boys for the destruction of sparrows, on which our fathers waged constant but apparently fruitless war. The problem of keeping birds out of the church exercised many churchwardens, and measures were taken to exclude 'pidgeons', 'owles' and 'crowes'. St. Martin's Leicester struggled for sixty-three years (1562–1625) against 'starlins', with results which are not recorded. Some parishes also maintained a dog-whipper, and a curious type of expanding dog-tongs is still extant.

All this parish business, important in the life of the village, was down to quite recent times intimately connected with the churches. Men could scarcely conceive of getting it done at all apart from the church. Nor, except during the glacial Puritan period, was the divorce between the church and the amusements of the village made completely effective until perhaps the middle of the nineteenth century. A game which must have been something like Eton fives was often played after morning service against the walls of the church itself. Verbal traditions survive of the rector umpiring, a fair return to those who had previously listened to his sermons. Jocelyn Jolliff's description of Dr. Rochecliff presiding over the village summer sports would probably fit many a country rector well enough for a century later.

Bell-ringing, in parishes fortunate enough to possess a peal, was both a sport and an art. It was necessarily connected with the church, though not nearly so closely as town-dwellers might suppose. To them the ringing of church bells is a summons to a church service. In a village it might be that or might not. It remains to-day the only surviving natural art of village people. Their music—their own untutored music—is gone. So is their dancing. So is their drama and their carol-singing. Superior people in the grip of antiquarian sentimentalism try to revive these things and call them 'folk', folk-music, folk-dancing and so forth, whatever they mean by that blessed word. Bell-ringing fortunately they have not yet touched, leaving its culture to the generations of ringers which have succeeded each other. The church accounts record plentifully the ringing of the bells for the comings and goings of the great. Failure to honour thus a royal visit or departure often caused the church doors to be sealed till a price was paid. Great events down the centuries were marked by pealing bells, such as 'the execucion of ye Quene of Scotts on scaffolde, js iiijd' (Stanford in the Vale, Berks, 1586), 'the great

Victorie against the spanyardes by the mightie hand of God, 8s' (St. Thomas Salisbury, 1588–9). The ringers might be rewarded by 'calves heddes' at Corpus Christi, or, as at Bristol, by an occasional day's duck-hunting.

They are sturdy, independent people even to-day, these ringers, not easily made amenable to discipline. They see no harm in a jug of beer in the tower itself after ringing for the King's birthday. Yet they are not irreverent or impious men. The following rhymed code of rules which long hung in the tower of a church well known to me shows the spirit in which they regard their work.

He that in ringing takes delight,
  And to the place draws near,
These articles, set in his sight,
  Must keep, if he rings here.

The first he must observe with care:
  Who comes within the door
Must, if he chance to curse or swear,
  Pay sixpence to the poor.

If any like to smoke or drink,
  They must not do so here:
Good reasons why—just let them think,
  This is GOD'S house of prayer.

He that his hat on's head doth keep
  Within this sacred place,
Must pay his sixpence ere he sleep,
  Or turn out in disgrace.

If any should our Parson sneer,
  Or warden's rules deride,
It is a rule of old, most clear,
  That such shan't here abide.

91 SOUTHWOLD, SUFFOLK: A STATELY EXAMPLE OF EAST ANGLIAN
FLINT FLUSHWORK

92 HOCKLEY CHURCH, ESSEX, AMONG ITS ROOK-HAUNTED ELMS

93 WILMINGTON, SUSSEX: A CORNER OF THE CHURCHYARD

The Sabbath Day we wish to keep
   And come to church and pray:
The man that breaks the ancient rule
   Shall never share our pay.

And when the bells are down and ceased
   It should be said or sung
And GOD preserve the Church and King
   And guide us safely Home.

Bell-ringing remains, half sport, half religious action, the single surviving example of the old connection between the village church and the people's amusements. It was as an amusement, perhaps as an art, that the Puritans disliked it. It is pathetic to think of John Bunyan, lurking at the foot of Elstow tower while the bells rang, wishing that he could take a rope along with his former comrades, but feeling that such indulgence was sinful. We find the same spirit of crabbed puritanism in the Rev. John Skinner, the 'Somerset Rector' whose journal Mr. Coombs edited and published. He quarrelled with his ringers and tried to prevent their ringing, for no reason apparently except that they enjoyed doing it. That was early in the nineteenth century.

It is curious to note how far we have travelled from the medieval uses of the village church, uses which stood for survival so long against the efforts of the reverent. I knew two old ladies, intensely and most beautifully religious, who protested repeatedly against the establishment of a tennis club in a field adjoining a churchyard. They feared that some balls, struck carelessly, might bounce against the wall, not of the church itself but of the churchyard. What would they have thought of the eighteenth-century fives players or the seventeenth-century drinkers of church ales?

It is interesting to speculate on the gradual triumph of the spirit of reverence—hypertrophied reverence?—over the natural desire of the village people to use their church for all purposes. We cannot lay the blame, or give the praise, entirely to the sixteenth-century reformers; the protests began long before their time. They did not apparently pay much attention to village churches, beyond destroying a few images of saints placed over porches and in other convenient places; and that was evidence of a spirit more set on belittling than exalting the sacredness of the 'temples made with hands'. The Puritans discountenanced the games and revels connected with the church, but that was because they disliked the games, certainly not because they wanted to emphasise the sanctity of the buildings which they called 'steeple houses'. The Wesleyans who built chapels of their own and used them for all sorts of purposes evidently did not feel strongly about the peculiar holiness of the buildings where God is worshipped. Perhaps the responsibility of the final victory of 'reverence' rests with the early Tractarians. It was they who persuaded us to sink our voices to whispers in church and to think that laughter is sacrilegious within the sacred walls. Yet it is odd that this almost excessive reverence should be the work of a party which later on was to be inspired by the idea of getting back to that England which was 'merrie England before the new learning came in'; when, in the village at all events, reverence was a less sensitive virtue than it is to-day and the church might boast with the Latin poet, '*Nihil humanum a me alienum puto*.'

The Reformation period, and even to a greater extent the Puritan aggression of the seventeenth century, were responsible for great changes inside our village churches. Many chancel screens were either demolished or suffered to fall into decay. Roods were invariably destroyed. Images of saints, set over porches or west doors, were often broken or defaced. Altars were moved from their positions at the east end of the church and set up as 'tables' elsewhere in the building. In Beckington, for instance, we read that the people had moved their altar and set it up 'on a mound' in the middle of the church. There it remained until Archbishop Laud appointed a commission of clergy from neighbouring parishes to see to it that the altar was restored to its proper place. But by far the worst damage done—worst because entirely irreparable—was the destruction of the fine stained glass which adorned the windows of our village churches. Here and there some of this glass survives, enough to sadden us with visions of all we have lost. For this the Puritans were much more responsible than the sixteenth-century reformers, who appear to have had little or no prejudice against stained glass. The Puritans, in spite of Milton's delight in 'storied windows richly dight', disliked it intensely and broke it where they could.

For one thing we may be thankful. Neither reformers nor Puritans interfered much with the actual fabric of the churches. That was left for the 'restorers' of the nineteenth century.

Of the two great religious revivals of the nineteenth century, the Evangelical took little or no interest in church-restoration. The Evangelicals built new churches —most of them deplorable—when they thought that new churches were wanted. This was for the most part in the suburbs of great cities where a rapidly growing population overflowed the original parish churches. But in the villages there was no such need and the Evangelicals left the village churches alone.

It was different when the Tractarian influence spread over the countryside, as it did very early in the history of the movement, in spite of episcopal frowns and the displeasure of those in high places. Thanks to the unfettered use of the right of private patronage, the new catholics obtained a footing in the parishes of rural England. They found their churches decayed and neglected by the long indifference of the eighteenth century. Possessed by a most laudable zeal to restore the glories of the ancient shrines, they wanted not only to rebuild what was falling into decay but to beautify the 'place of the sanctuary' and render it once again fit for catholic worship.

Unfortunately they did not know how to set about the work; few men in mid-Victorian times understood the spirit of the old architecture. Yet every zealous priest and earnest churchwarden was ready to step in where even well-educated angels might have feared to tread. The result was a series of 'restorations' which have become proverbial for their artistic failure, which might induce a pious antiquary to say in despair that he would have preferred a new Puritanism to the energy of Anglo-Catholicism.

Yet it is quite possible to exaggerate the evil done by the nineteenth-century restorers, even though they obliterated mural paintings which they found covered with whitewash, filled the churches with furniture designed in the worst tradition of the sham antique, and put abominable glass into the naked windows. Sometimes, though not often, they respected the actual fabric of the church. Where they touched that the results were truly disastrous; but in the villages, perhaps for want of money, they seldom did.

It has become the fashion of late years—a very praiseworthy fashion—to post in the church lists of the names of the rectors or vicars from the earliest possible date. These names are taken from the diocesan records and may be regarded as reliable, though the dates of the beginnings and endings of the earlier incumbencies are sometimes doubtful. An interesting feature of such lists is the change which appears in the nature of the names. Up to the fourteenth century it is observed that the names are chiefly Norman French, often adorned with the prefix 'de'. Afterwards names of Saxon origin appear more frequently, which would go to show a gradual advance in the education and social position of the English people. But the evidence here is too scanty and uncertain to justify any definite conclusion being drawn. What is much more certain is that the lists show no signs of a break of continuity in the church life of the villagers in the sixteenth century. The same priest lived through long stretches of the Reformation period apparently undisturbed either by his own conscience or by the action of external authority.

In one of our village churches some years ago an artist was employed to decorate a wooden screen erected across the west end of the church, set up to shut off the choir vestry. She—the artist was a lady—conceived the rather original idea of adorning the screen with small busts, purely imaginary of course, of the rectors who held the living in past times. Among others was a man who had survived the period of the chief Reformation changes without, apparently, being in any way disturbed. The artist, who had a sense of humour, represented him, 'Studying the New Prayer Book'. At the time this work was done we were all more or less excited about the Prayer Book of 1928, which was called the 'New' Prayer Book. The artist—and she may very well have been right—thought there was a likeness between the changes then suggested and those of the Reformation. In 1928 people in high places, bishops, archdeacons, members of convocation and, for some obscure reason, many politicians (men who had never before shown any interest in the Church), became intensely excited, debated, voted, and appealed to God and Holy Scriptures. The priests and people in the villages remained entirely unmoved. They saw no reasons to get excited about changes which were not going to affect them. The village people simply knew nothing about it and cared nothing either one way or the other. Was this, as the artist supposed, what happened to the Reformation? Was it too an affair of excited politicians, angry bishops, and statesmen attached to this doctrine or that? Were the villagers and their churches as little affected, as unwilling to 'take sides', as they were in 1928? The evidence of the lists of incumbents would go to suggest this, as well as some of the wardens' accounts.

Though the rapid and revolutionary changes must have proved bewildering to plain church folk, altars, roods, and images seem to have been destroyed, replaced, and finally removed in the most matter-of-fact way. At St. Mary Devizes the triple transformation was effected in the eleven years between 1550 and 1561, while at Ashburton, Devon, the rood, with 'Mary and John', was set up in 1545–6, taken down and burnt two years later, replaced some ten years after, and finally pulled to pieces in 1559–60. But St. Martin Leicester provides probably the fullest and most interesting account of the wholesale disposal of the rich and varied furniture, the replacement by cheaper substitutes under Mary, and a second clearing away after Elizabeth's accession. Here the same man, Sexton, was employed both to set up the rood and destroy it. The provision of service books tells an equally exciting tale, which resulted in the missal, processional, manual, and the rest being replaced by the Bible (spelt in different accounts Bybyll, bybull, or byble), Book of Common Prayer, Paraphrase of Erasmus, Foxe's *Book of Martyrs* and Bishop Jewel's *Apology for the Church of England*.

The Reformation then did not apparently affect the English villagers and their services in any revolutionary manner. In the latter the changes made in the church services came gradually and in a certain sense locally. A village where the sympathies of the parson, and, one must add, the squire were Protestant, would make changes rapidly and drastically. A village in which the predominating persons were conservative would, during the early stages of the Reformation at least, change but little. In neither case was there anything like a violent revolution. This tolerant apathy in the face of change was not, of course, universal. The Pilgrims of Grace in the North and certain disturbances in the extreme South-west witness to the fact that many people in these districts were profoundly moved and deeply resentful of doctrinal changes and, perhaps still more, of changes in the ritual and ornaments of their services and churches. But for the most part there was little sign that either priests or people in the villages took very much notice of what was going on. Their church was their church. They had built it, cared for it, been proud of it, loved it. It remained their church whatever Henry VIII said about the Pope or the Pope said about Queen Elizabeth.

The Puritan dominance of England was a very different business. The priest to whom the people were accustomed, whom perhaps they respected and loved, was driven from his office, or held it with the utmost difficulty at the cost of self-respect. Dark tales circulated about the treatment of these dispossessed clergy in prison hulks and elsewhere. Stern Puritan pastors, often men of

94 A DISTANT VIEW OF KESWICK, LOOKING TO SKIDDAW, CUMBERLAND

95   THE OLD POST MILL AT HOLTON STREET, SUFFOLK

intense devotion and great ability but entirely without breeding or social authority, preached doctrines which sounded strange in the ears of mild English rustics. A real revolution was attempted in the churches and villages of rural England—was attempted but failed. There remained, after the tyranny was past, only a little widening of the division which the Reformation began between the church life and the secular life of rural England. Never again was the church so visibly and undeniably the centre of all village life.

After the Restoration the people came back to the church, as to a familiar home. And even to-day when, as we shall see, the spirit of nonconformity has found a place in village life, there remains a feeling that a baptism is not quite a baptism, a marriage a little dubious, and a funeral lacking in proper respect to the dead, unless the Church plays her part. A dissenter, most eager in the support of his sect, will yet bring his baby to be baptized in the parish church, will seek the Church's blessing for his daughter at her marriage, and expect, when he dies, to be laid in the ground consecrated by the Church which during his life he avoided. On two other occasions and two only will the ardent village dissenter take willing part in the church service. A great event of State—a coronation, a royal Jubilee, or the funeral of a monarch—draws men of all opinions to their parish church. The annual thanksgiving for the blessings of harvest finds even the most vigorous dissenter among the church's worshippers. So much at least remains of the old conception, too deeply rooted to be easily or quickly destroyed, that Church and State are inseparable and that our differences of theological opinion are trivial things compared with the procession of the year, spring-time and harvest, summer and winter, day and night.

Dissent and nonconformity in the village came into existence largely as the result of the preaching of John Wesley, though some sects like the 'Independents' and Quakers are of far earlier origin. Wesley was himself a priest of the Church of England, and, as it seems, never contemplated a schism of any kind. Many of his earlier followers were of his mind, and for a long time there remained a number of what were called Church Methodists, who, though they worshipped apart on all ordinary occasions, went to their parish churches on great festivals and there, headed by their minister, received the sacrament. But circumstances were too strong for those who felt any kind of loyalty to the Church from which they sprang. Partly through the fault of the Church, partly because the old bottles could not be stretched to contain the fermenting new wine, schism became inevitable.

New buildings were required where men might express as seemed right to them the devotion of their hearts. Side by side with the old parish churches there sprang up all over rural England Methodist chapels. They survive to-day and almost everywhere are in violent contrast with the old churches. Built as the expression of the religious fervour of the people; built by the people in their own manner, out of their own resources; their origin is very like that of the parish churches. But, unlike the churches, they are strangely devoid of any kind of beauty. It is not merely that they lack or for a long time lacked the mellowing of age which does confer on what was not originally beautiful a sort of pleasing aroma of the past. No passing of years could beautify these buildings. They are irremedially ugly. Neither is their ugliness due entirely to lack of education in their congregations—the Church of England fabrics of the same date cry equally to heaven with their hideousness (think, in Hertfordshire, of Ayot St. Peter compared with North Mimms). It is as evident as it is lamentable that the spontaneous spirit of beautiful crafts-manship, the innate taste that pervaded all the Middle Ages and lingered on until the eighteenth century, had vanished like a dream. It is vain to plead that these churches and chapels were often built by the poor and that rich ornament or stately grandeur were impossible. Beauty does not depend on rich ornament and can exist where there is no stateliness. Many of our old churches are very simple and quite plainly the work of poor men. Yet their beauty delights us. . . .

But are we, even those of us who are most devoted to the vanishing beauty of our villages, right in railing at the ugliness which offends us in chapels, cottages, schools, and village halls?

> Ah me! with wider vision
> Perhaps I should forgive
> The horrid little houses
> Where happy people live.

Ivor Brown

THE
INN

Once the word 'Inn' was a synonym for 'house'. The great Earl of Warwick's London house was Warwick Inn. The lawyers had their Inns and in their territory the old name remains. The students had Inns. But the commonest Inn was the house common to all who could pay for its services, the house by the side of the road. The Road House is now a new term for a very old thing, but it signifies a new kind of tavern, being the simple description of a sophisticated place. In a Road House one does not expect to find tosspot tinkers with their ale, but smart young people with their Gin-and-Its. Since smart young people affect the games of the populace, there will be opportunities for throwing the democratic dart and shoving, with manicured hands, the democratic halfpenny. There will be a bathing-pool to cool the bodies of those who have taken no more exercise than is demanded by changing gears and pressing

96 'THE GEORGE', DORCHESTER-ON-THAMES: A FINE OLD INN ON THE OXFORD ROAD

97 THE 'LION', SHREWSBURY: A SUBSTANTIAL GEORGIAN HOSTELRY ON THE ROAD TO WALES

pedals. Information will probably be given that, for health's sake, the waters of the pool have been chemically treated; something similar may have happened to the alcoholic refreshment, but the fact will have less publicity.

The new Road House is interesting to all who are interested in the sway and movement of tradition. It is not catering, as did the old inn or tavern, for those who must use the road and therefore need a house of call to break their journey and refresh their bodies. It is alluring people on to the road to enjoy the pleasure of a house set thereby. It is not a relief for country wayfarers but a recreation for town-workers. You do not plod on to find a Road House at the end of the day's journey, but seek it out for what fun it may contain.

The Road House, then, belongs to the age of quick and easy movement, whereas the inn was the product of slow and arduous travel. At the Road House, the visitor, having journeyed lightly by the power of mechanical horses, immediately starts to be active, to take exercise on the dancing floor, in the water, on the miniature golf-course, or at lawn tennis. At the traditional English inn the traveller tumbled from the top of a coach in a half-frozen state or rolled exhausted off his horse in order to be restored with hot brandy and water and hot cuts from the joint. He sat by the fire and drank punch until it was time to be in bed. The pleasures were sedentary and narcotic. Men drank and conversed; cards and chess might be played; nothing more strenuous, unless love be deemed laborious. Love, indeed, could lead to strenuous complications, as the adventures of Tom Jones in the inn at Upton remind us. But, on the whole, the journey was an ordeal and the inn a mitigation. If not a good inn it was a sorrow's crown of sorrow, and many English travellers have bitterly recorded their opinion of the tavern as the home of tribulation. The phrase 'a blackguard stop' is a common grunt of displeasure in the Torrington Diaries, and many an English inn of the 'Good Old Days' evoked similar curses from the fatigued and hungry patron.

The first English Road House presumably appeared with the first English roads. Assuming these to be the ridgeways over the downland grass which lead up from the Channel harbours to the great centres of the megalithic culture, we may imagine the earliest English inn as an establishment in Dorset, set by one of the green tracks used by the ancient mariners from the Mediterranean who were filtering in nearly four thousand years ago to make their Wiltshire capital and their cathedral cities of Avebury and Stonehenge. As capitals naturally attract litigants and people busy on affairs of State, and as cathedral cities naturally provide shelter for pilgrims, both are richly clustered with inns; so the original headquarters of the catering trade must have lain thereabouts. If inns had signs and titles then (and why should they not?) 'The Rising Sun' was probably the name of the first English pub. Or was our 'Beetle and Wedge' anticipated by the 'Flint and Scraper'?

But these fancies need not delay us; nor need we retrace in any detail the history of the English inn from the Roman *taberna* to the cosmopolitan Grand Babylon.

The tale has been told often enough; what, perhaps, has been less often done is to view the inn in terms of its function, a method already suggested by the distinction between the inn, serving busy travellers on the road, and the Road House, creating idle ones. The inn has continually expanded its activities; it has been club and theatre as well as ale-house and purveyor of bread and cheese. It has been an important centre for commercial meetings and transactions, a petty forum for the discussion of public affairs, and a compendium of games. Originating to provide material relief from the rigours of the road, it soon began to add a few simple amusements, but nothing so elaborate, of course, as the sporting, swimming, and dancing of the modern Road House.

It is possible that, when the Roman soldier tramped the roads which his subject-races and auxiliary troops had so laboriously made under his directions, the *tabernarius* of the district provided knuckle-bones as well as liquor, gave him targets at which to throw the mimic *tela* or darts, or installed in his bar a board for shoving the *semi-denarius*. It is certain that in the Middle Ages and later the patron of the ale-house might expect to find the requirements for a game of chess. Under 'Chequers' the *Oxford English Dictionary* announces 'a chess-board as the sign of an inn, the name of a public house, Middle English'. Most Oxford men, who knew their way about, must at one time have taken Matthew Arnold's hint to view 'the stripling Thames at Bablock Hythe'. If they did so, walking down over Cumnor Hurst or rowing up by way of Upper River, they surely had found thirst enough to visit the Chequers Inn. Probably they omitted to play chess. But chess gave the title to the numerous Chequers Inns of England; the house-fronts were often painted with a chequer design to announce the game within.

If we follow the sporting aspect of the inn down the centuries we notice a continual widening of the programme until we reach the luxurious modern holiday hotel with its tennis-courts, private golf-course, swimming-pool, dance-hall, and various gymnastic appliances. The inn of the humbler kind, both urban and rural, usually offers darts, shove-halfpenny, and dominoes; cards it is forbidden to allow, lest gaming ensue. The games just mentioned are usually played for no greater stake than a round of drinks, but I have seen money pass over dominoes. There are other public-house games which involve more exertion. Skittles, for example, not only demands long practice and prodigies of skill but considerable strength as well. The 'cheese', as the missile is called which is propelled at the ninepins, is a heavy object with which most beginners will be unable even to reach the target. The adroitness of the experienced skittler is staggering. He can put a twist on the 'cheese' as he throws it which will cause it to break on landing and so curve round the board on which the nine pins are set, knocking them down in turn. The greatest skill is needed when two or three pins only are standing and these are widely separated. It is astonishing to see the way in which a master-hand can fell them at a single shot by spinning the 'cheese' from one to another.

In darts too there is uncanny certainty of aim, and great competitions are held in which teams from various inns compete.

Both in town and country the inn is sometimes possessed of a bowling-green, which adds decoration to amusement. What lovelier, for instance, than the garden of the Falcon Inn at Painswick in the Cotswolds, fine house of a fine stone town in a fine rolling country where the woolmen made their fortunes once and left their testament in building? The bowling-green of the 'Falcon' always lives in my memory as the perfection of a tavern's side-lines. Here is the English lawn amid the English scene, both at the green pinnacle of beauty. And what a relief to find behind some of the larger urban or sub-urban public-houses the smooth and velvety expanse of a well-kept bowling-green! It reminds one of the full function of the inn, which is to be a meeting-place for all pleasure, a spot where sport is mellowed with refresh-ment. Inns often have their own bowling-teams who go forth to meet their opposites, sampling a rival liquor and a rival turf. Quite close to my own home in Hamp-stead there is an inn, the 'Freemason's Arms', at the bottom of Downshire Hill, which preserves in its garden an old Dutch game called 'Mell'. This involves rolling large wooden balls through a pivoting iron hoop in the centre of the pitch; the balls are lifted and jerked forward with long poles which have a ring at the end of them. The hoop through which they must pass is very little larger than the balls and is continually swinging about; the accuracy of aim displayed is remarkable and, with the garden illuminated on a summer night to make the game possible after sunset, it is a pleasant spectacle for those who only sit, sip, and stare. The trees throw strange shadows and the wind whispers leafily amid the traffic and banter and hospitality of the game. It seems a long way from tubes, nearer to some rustic heaven than to Charing Cross.

The inns of less humane centuries than our own were often centres of various combative and baiting sports, if sport is a proper name for such barbarities. The 'Dog and Badger' tells its own story. So does the 'Dog and Bear', a common title in the eighteenth century. The 'Dog and Duck', a house of disorderly character in St. George's Fields, had a pond in which spaniels pursued ducks. The duck might make an escape by continual diving, the dog waiting for its reappearance. The 'Cock' and the 'Fighting Cocks' are common inn-names and self-explanatory of the fun provided. The 'cock-shy' was an even beastlier amusement than the cock-fight. The player paid so much for the right to throw a billet at a cock tied to a stake; if he killed it outright the bird was the player's property, to take home for dinner; if not, he lost his stake-money. A man need not take his prize, but could sell it back to the publican. Larwood and Hotten, in their excellent book on *The History of Signboards*, quote the following from a paper of 1700:

'Last Tuesday a Brewer's servant in Southwark took his walk round Towerhill, Moorfield, and Lincoln's Inn Fields, and knocked down so many cocks that by selling them again he returned home twenty shillings odd pence richer man than he came out.'

Many Bear Inns have their origin in baiting-pits which attracted custom, but one 'Bear', in the Strand, was a centre of scholarship. The Society of Antiquaries was founded there in 1707. The humanitarian movements of the nineteenth century gradually ended the more brutal aspects of tavern sport and replaced the tethered cock with the nine-pins, the bear-pit with the bowling-green.

The inn was also a nursery of English acting, and, as such, dictated the architecture of the first English theatres. The miracle-plays of the Middle Ages were acted on a wheeled platform. The wagon of Thespis, the traditional father of Greek drama, was thus employed again in the sacred mummings of the English craftsmen. The plays or pageants were drawn round the town when a mystery 'cycle' was being given. At Chester, wrote an archdeacon of the fifteenth century,

'They first began at the Abbaye Gates . . . then it was wheeled to the Highe Cross before the Mayor. Before that was donne, the seconds came and the firste went to Watergate Street and from thence to the Bridge Street and soe all, one after another, till all the pageantes weare played.'

When drama became secularised what more natural than that the moving spectacle should be carried to the inn-yards whose galleries were so perfectly adapted to the needs of an audience? If you go into one of the galleried taverns, such as the New Inn at Gloucester, you feel at once that the place is a natural amphitheatre. Juliet should appear upon that balcony and the minstrels likewise be aloft. Malvolio should strut here and be mocked by the rogues in hiding among the timbers. When the theatre architect began to build regular play-houses he accepted the tradition of the inn-yard play-boys. The first English professional theatres were direct descendants of the hostelry into whose court the players had drawn their platform and properties. A platform, with a pent-house, arose as it were amid the galleries of a tavern, which surrounded this platform-stage almost entirely. The lords, ladies, and wealthy patrons went to occupy seats aloft. The groundlings stood in the relics of the coach-yard. Dramatists must compose their plays to suit their premises, and the free-and-easy motion and the rhetorical splendour of the Elizabethan drama were conditioned by the large platform-stage, absence of frontal curtain, and lack of roof in the theatres which had sprung from the inn-yard. Consequently, it is no exaggeration to say that, among the many gifts brought to English life by the English inn, was the cut and shape of Shakespeare's plays.

During the nineteenth century the tavern was once more a home of theatrical enterprise. The existence of the 'patent', which restricted drama of quality to the authorised houses of the West End, drove intending players to find non-theatrical premises. These lesser stages were set in a garden, as at the 'Yorkshire Stingo' in the Marylebone Road, or in a hall behind the saloon,

98 THE NOONDAY INTERVAL AT THE 'PLOUGH AND HARROW', LITLINGTON, SUSSEX

99 THE 'TRAVELLERS' REST': A LITTLE LAKELAND INN ON THE SUMMIT OF
THE KIRKSTONE PASS, WESTMORLAND

as at the 'Rosemary Branch' in Hoxton. It was through these tavern-theatres that the French romantic drama and *opera bouffe* filtered into England. Dumas and Hugo were made available, along with pots of ale, for a few pence by the theatre-minded publicans. The 'Grecian', in the City Road, was famous for its musical shows. It was illegal to play Shakespeare in these places, but, strange as it may seem to-day, the public thirst for Shakespeare equalled the public thirst for liquor, and the inn-keepers were actually tempted to smuggle Shakespeare! The proprietors of the Union Saloon in Shoreditch were actually brought before the justices and fined for purveying *Othello* on the sly.

On page 200 is a typical bill of the Victorian tavern-theatre. (The Britannia Tavern was the parent of the Britannia Theatre.)

The publican certainly offered value for money, when he presented all this dramatic fare plus refreshment for a shilling. It was from the smoking-concerts of similar tavern-theatres that the English music-hall developed; there was a chairman in charge of the proceedings, ready to call for order, and announce the next singer. The smoking-concert of the inn remained a nursery of vaudeville talent for many years; many of the north-country comedians learned their job in licensed premises. A famous house in this respect was the Slip Inn in the old centre of Manchester.

So much for the inn as the centre of entertainment; it has naturally served also as a centre of commerce. The English market town is always thickly set with inns, and

THE ROYAL BRITANNIA SALOON AND BRITANNIA THEATRE

Proprietor: Mr. S. Lane
Licensed pursuant to Act of Parliament

Will open on EASTER MONDAY and every evening
with an entirely new Melodrama of
extraordinary interest

THE RED LANCE

OR, THE MERRIE MEN OF HOXTON

———

Powerful Dramatic Company
Elaborate Scenic Effects

GRAND CONCERT AND VAUDEVILLE
including MISS PEARCE

BALLET
introducing the famous Pantomime Dancer
FLEXMORE

The whole of this gigantic entertainment
concluding with the laughable farce

THE TAILOR OF TADWORTH

———

Doors open at 6 p.m.   Commence 6.30 p.m.
Upper Circle 1*s.*—for which a
Refreshment Ticket is given
Reserved Seats 6*d.*

GOD SAVE THE QUEEN

these were used not only for refreshment after the sale of the livestock in the pens outside but for the clinching of suggested bargains or the making of new ones. In the town the inn or hotel is the home of the commercial traveller for five days in the week, and the frequent advertisement of 'capacious stock-rooms' shows that he makes the inn his show-case as well as his dining-room and dormitory. The inn was the natural place for a man in search of business to appoint for meetings with his clients. It also became the resort of quacks and of fortune-tellers and the showmen of freaks. The learned women, who usually proclaimed themselves to be the seventh daughters of seventh daughters, would take a room at a tavern there to practise their gifts of divination, interpreting of dreams, and the like. Here is a bill of 1667.

'At Mr. Croome's, at the sign of the Shoe and Slap, near the Hospital Gate, in West Smithfield, is to be seen

THE WONDER OF NATURE

A Girl above Sixteen Years of Age, born in Cheshire, and not above Eighteen inches long, having shed her Teeth several Times, and not a perfect Bone in any Part of her, only the Head, yet she hath all her senses to Admiration, and Discourses, Reads very well, Sings, Whistles, and all very pleasant to hear.'

(The slap, by the way, was a form of slipper.)

Another notice of 1718 is typical of the tavern's function as a dubious drug-store.

'The Anodyne Necklace for children's teeth, women in labour, and distempers of the head; price 5s. Recommended by Dr. Chamberlain. Sold up one pair of stairs at the sign of the Anodyne Necklace, without Temple Bar; at the Spanish Lady at the Royal Exchange, next Threadneedle Street; at the Indian Handkerchief, facing the New Stairs in Wapping, etc.'

The eighteenth-century inns did much miscellaneous trafficking; bottles of liquor more salutary than fiery were on sale along with the regular stock-in-trade. The chalybeate waters of Hampstead, for example, from which Well Walk takes its name, were not only drunk by visitors to the suburb; they were bottled and sold in many of the London taverns. To-day the country innkeeper may be a grocer, confectioner, and tobacconist, running a profitable side-line in potato-crisps and bars of chocolate. The inn as a place of professional meeting was immemorably exemplified in fiction by the sessions of Mr. Wackford Squeers at the 'Saracen's Head' on Snow Hill, where Mr. Snawley deposited his step-children and Mr. Nicholas Nickleby was engaged as gentleman-usher, although Mr. Squeers had gravely remarked that the absence of a college degree was a strong objection to an engagement at Dotheboys Hall. And nowadays the Grand Babylons are the scenes of innumerable 'deals' on the grand scale. Parents need not attend the Savoy Grill in order to talk business with the Head Master of Eton, but on such premises many plans have been laid, many syndicates formed, many plays launched, many books contracted for, and many transactions in real estate have been settled. The face that launched a thousand films may be in Hollywood or Elstree; but the finances behind the face (and considerably more important) may have been secured in the dining-room of the Hotel Magnificent. To the great hotels come the great visitors, there to be called upon by the Press and to deliver to the assembled reporters a few halting remarks which they may be surprised to discover as imposing, important, and exclusive interviews on the following morning.

The inn, as we have seen, was architecturally the parent of the early English theatre and in spirit the parent of the English music-hall. It was also the ancestor of an institution especially dear to the English, the club. The Bread Street 'Mermaid' has been described as the headquarters of a Mermaid Club, instituted by Sir Walter Raleigh and including Shakespeare, Beaumont, Fletcher, and many poets and wits of the period. There is ample evidence that the lively fellows of the time met at the 'Mermaid' for refreshment and for repartee, but that a formal club existed is doubtful. The usage of the word is not Elizabethan or Jacobean. It was not until half a century later that Aubrey wrote: 'We now use the word clubbe for a sodality in a tavern.' Aubrey joined the Rota, a political club meeting at the 'Turk's Head' in New Palace Yard, and Pepys talks of Wood's in Pall Mall as 'our old house for clubbing'. The Mall became in time the great club street, and the eighteenth century coffee-houses also became the parents of many famous clubs. What is certain is that the inn served a public need of a wide kind, being the home of intellectual and social as well of commercial exchanges in the Elizabethan period. Beaumont is explicit about the 'Mermaid' as the anvil of the sparking wits; the walls echoed with

> the words that have been
> So nimble and so full of subtle flame
> As if that every one from whence they came
> Had meant to put his whole wit in a jest
> And had resolved to live a fool the rest
> Of his dull life.

The Shakespeare group met at the 'Mermaid'; the rival sodality of Ben Jonson were at the 'Devil', between Temple Bar and Middle Temple Gate, which had a large upper room known as 'The Oracle of Apollo', with the god's bust and the assurance that 'Truth itself doth flow in wine'. Ben was a great focus of tavern company and tavern wit; whenever he sat at the 'Devil', the 'Sun', the 'Dog', or the 'Triple Tun', the young men gathered round to hear the news and banter of the day. There was learning too, for Selden, Cotton, Camden, and Donne were good tavern-men.

The aristocrats of the eighteenth century did not disdain to meet in simple taverns for their 'clubbing'. The most notable instance of great men in small places was afforded by the Kit-Kat Club. This was founded by a group of Whig nobles including six dukes and five earls as well as such great names in politics and letters as those of Walpole, Vanbrugh, Congreve, and Addison. They met in a small and shabby house by Temple Bar, kept by Christopher Katt, a notable pie-man whose articles took

100 THE 'PINEAPPLE', ASHFORD HILL, BERKSHIRE: A ROADSIDE COTTAGE-ALEHOUSE

101 'UNSOPHISTICATED ALES AND STOUT': THE LITTLE 'LEATHER
BOTTLE' AT COBHAM, KENT, KNOWN TO MR. PICKWICK, BEFORE
ITS RESTORATION

his name, as sandwiches were named after the Earl of Sandwich. He also bestowed an abiding title on the renowned gentry who ate, drank, and talked upon his premises. The Kit-Kat gallants scratched the names of fair ladies on the tavern glasses and wrote verses to the toasts. In summer the members preferred the brisker air of Hampstead, and drove out to celebrate their revels at the 'Upper Flask' on the summit of the hill, not far from the present 'Jack Straw's Castle', recently a great resort of boxing, music-hall, and sporting folk. The 'clubbers' of the eighteenth century included the sages, philosophers, and men of science as well as the political grandees and literary wits. The Royal Society Club, for instance, or, as it was originally called, the Club of Royal Philosophers, was founded at the 'King's Arms' in St. Paul's Churchyard and subsequently moved to the 'Mitre' in Fleet Street, 'over against Fetter Lane'. Later meeting-places of this august body were at the Crown and Anchor Tavern in the Strand and the 'Freemasons' in Great Queen Street.

There is no space here to follow up the intricate and amusing history of clubs and sodalities. The inn deserves to be honoured for its share in English politics, letters, and scholarship; the public-house of the eighteenth century was a valuable part of public life. Certainly it collected the scamps and baggages of the town; equally it lured the wits and poets and has continued to do so, though in decreasing measure. Where Macheath tippled and wenched, a Dr. Halley might be combining science of the mind with solace of the body. The 'Salutation and Cat' in Newgate Street had a long tradition of literary assemblage, and it was in one of its little upper rooms that Coleridge and Lamb smoked and drank and discussed the salvation of mankind by Pantisocracy. The 'cat', in this case, was the name of a snuff-box concealed in the knob of a cane. One gentleman would salute another with a flourish and offer him the 'cat'. The decline of the tavern as a forge and anvil for the heat and sparkle of the mind came during the nineteenth century, when the 'clubbers' set up for themselves in their own premises. Scholarship occupied the Athenaeum, and the mansion by Decimus Burton was opened in 1830. Gentlemen interested in the Theatre founded the Garrick a few years later, and the Savage was a mid-Victorian foundation for a group of artists and professional men who planted the sea-coast of Bohemia on Adelphi Terrace. In the eighteenth century all such fraternities, including the most learned and severe, would have met in taverns or in coffee-houses. The tradition of the inn as a place for mixing wit with liquor has remained in certain Fleet Street bars, at the 'Fitzroy' and the 'Plough' in the Bloomsbury area, and at the 'Cadogan Arms' and other taverns of the Chelsea colony. The 'Café Royal' at the southern end of Regent Street took over and to some extent retains the legacy of the wits' sparking-ground—with ladies present.

The inn as meeting-place naturally provokes and enriches the conversation most natural to its visitors. So, while the poets and politicals attended the Kit-Kat and the blades of the town were eating and jesting at the Society of Beefsteaks, the humbler citizens of the eighteenth century were discussing their affairs of trade and sport in their own taverns. And so it continues. At the 'Miners' Arms' there will be consideration of the miner's wage; in the tap-room of the country inn one still may discover what price a score of ewes, a likely suggestion for a horse-race, or the countryside's opinion of the Prime Minister. But here again the club has interfered with the prosperity of the inn. The foundation of working men's clubs has been encouraged by a ridiculous complication of our laws, which make it possible to obtain a club-licence easily and for a few shillings, while a tavern-licensee must pass the strictest interrogations of the police and pay heavily for the right to retail his spirits, wines, ales, and tobaccos. Some village inns have been seriously damaged by the licensed club-rooms of the British Legion, and many urban ones have felt the severe competition of political and social clubs, which avoid the heavy taxation imposed upon the publican. None the less, if, on arrival in a strange place, you want to understand its commerce and to discover the public opinion of the locality, a quiet session in a bar with an attentive ear will probably yield authentic information about the traffic of the district and the views of its inhabitants on first things as well as on last. I have listened to a very brisk discussion on the immortality of the soul in a moorland tavern of the north; this debate followed immediately on one no less brisk about the advisability of crossing Swaledale sheep with Cheviots. One remembers Pepys at Salisbury. 'The master of the house was a sober, understanding man and I had good discourse with him about this country's matters as wool, corn, and other things.' The inn remains the forum which it was to the Hanoverian statesmen when they carried their politics as well as their thirsts to the 'Upper Flask'. Other folk, other issues; the tendency of alcohol to promote omniscient airs continues delightfully to give fire to argument and confidence to wild assertion.

But, after all, the major business of the inn is to provide sustenance and shelter. In the Middle Ages the walls of cities were realities and the gates might be barriers. The traveller arriving after dark might find entrance impossible, but he would be able to find wine and warmth in the taverns which naturally grew up just outside the walls as a refuge for the late-comer. That explains the rich deposit of inns on the south bank of the Thames. Southwark was the place where the wayfarer could be sure of hospitality; he could lie at the 'Tabard' until such time as the City of London were ready to admit him. Whether he lay clean was another matter, but fussing over cleanliness is, after all, only a modern habit. Pepys, after his talk with the sober, understanding man of Salisbury, reports 'beds good but lousy, which made us merry'. Nowadays we are not so easily amused.

The kind of picture which used to be given away with Illustrated Christmas Supplements wonderfully idealised the England of the pack-horse and the coach. 'Mine hoste' was depicted red as a berry in the face and as white as snow in the linen; his fires glowed and roared, his table was stocked with joints of equal size and

102 THE 'CROWN', HEMPSTEAD, ESSEX: THE BIRTHPLACE OF DICK TURPIN

103 THE 'GEORGE', KIMBOLTON, HUNTINGDONSHIRE, ADJOINING
THE CASTLE GATES

104 THE 'TALBOT', RIPLEY, SURREY: THE COACH ENTRANCE

succulence, his pewter sparkled, and everybody seemed to be at the summit of health, heartiness, and happiness. The records of the English travellers often give flat denial to this vision of convivial bliss; they frequently record shabby, verminous inns and sulky, incompetent proprietors. The proverbial Boniface might more accurately have been called Bughouse. However, there are bright reports to set beside the snarls and lamentations of those who lay down empty and remained to scratch. Naturally the resources of the inn depended on the likely amount of patronage. The hostelry on a big coaching-road could rely upon the regular arrival of customers and so had its preparations made, the kettle steaming for the punch and negus, the ostlers and waiters ready, the bread fresh, and the meats set forth in appetising abundance. At any rate, by the time we reach 'Tom Brown' on the road to Rugby we can rely on good service on the Rugby road. There would be a hideously early start, but what a welcome and what a breakfast after thirty-five miles of bleak exposure!

'There is the low dark wainscoted room, hung with sporting-prints; the hat-stand (with a whip or two standing up in it belonging to bagmen who are still in bed) by the door; the blazing fire, with the quaint old glass over the mantelpiece, in which is stuck a large card with the list of the meets for the week of the county hounds. The table, covered with the whitest of cloths and of china, and bearing a pigeon pie, ham, round of cold boiled beef cut from a mammoth ox, and the great loaf of household bread on a wooden trencher. And here comes in the stout head waiter, puffing under a tray of hot viands; kidneys and a steak, transparent rashers and poached eggs, buttered toast and muffins, coffee and tea, all smoking hot. The table can never hold it all.'

That must be set against the dismal records of English inns to be found in the travel records of Taylor the Water-Poet, in the log of Celia Fiennes, or in the grumblings of the Torrington Diaries.

The English inn of to-day receives much criticism. It is such a various institution that generalisation becomes absurd. It includes the cottage with a beer-licence and a front room as improvised bar, the fully licensed house whose owner is free to sell a Burton beer as well as the local product, and the far commoner 'tied house', an inn owned by a brewery and constrained to sell only that brewery's draught ales. The 'tied houses' outnumber the free by at least ten to one. All these may be rather houses of call than houses of prolonged visitation. The inn then reaches upward to become the commercial house or country tavern with a dining-room and beds to let. After that come the various grades of hotel.

The fanatical enemies of the inn like to talk about 'drink-shops', just as they are always describing as 'consuming alcohol' or as 'a victim of the Liquor Traffic' the man who only deems himself to be having a quiet pint of beer. Well, the ale-house is a drink-shop, but since to sell drinks is a legitimate occupation it is none the worse for that. What matters is the quality of the drink and the pleasantness of the shop. The former, since the house is usually 'tied', will depend on the suitability of the local water for brewing and the skill of the local brewer. Here tastes differ so much as to make wide judgment impossible. What can be said on behalf of the 'tied' house is that the system keeps brewing a diversified and dispersed occupation, not a bad thing in a world of centralisation and monotony. Nearly every English rural district has its local brewery; often the beer is inferior to that made at Burton-on-Trent, whose abbey in the time of Cœur-de-Lion was already renowned for its ale.

> The Abbot of Burton brewed good ale
> On Fridays, when they fasted.

According to Hackwood, in his *Inns and Ales of Old England*,

'It must by no means be thought that the pre-eminence of Burton ale has been derived by brewing it from the inexhaustible waters of the Trent; the secret of its success lay in the peculiar suitability of the water supplied by its numerous wells, the chemical or natural properties of which confer those potable qualities so much approved by the connoisseur. The water passes through some gypsum beds in the neighbourhood.'

Hackwood further relates that at Burton a village carrier called Bass started to brew in his home in 1723. He did well enough to make brewing his mainstay. So he sold his carter's business to a family called Pickford. Both houses have been heard of since.

If there were open competition in beer the Burton brews would probably destroy a great many local breweries and so displace labour in places where industry is already small and waning. The 'tied house' system is conferring some benefit in a country where the multiple store is continually harassing and even ruining the small trader. Often there is competition between two local brewers or between two houses serving the product of one, so that lack of initiative and of will to please are usually penalised. The worst kind of inn, slovenly and conducted by a sluttish landlord, may occur in the small village where he has a monopoly. Expecting few visitors who may want food with their drink, he is ready for none, and will only offer bread and cheese with a bad grace.

The efficiency and cheerfulness of the village inn naturally depend to some extent on the amount of custom. It is rarely, in rural districts, a drink-shop merely, since, as we have seen, it is the centre of gossip, discussion, and indoor and outdoor games. Its tenant probably organises a thrift club whose members draw their savings at Christmas, and a summer outing, for which coppers are put by week by week. The amount of rural drunkenness is trifling; the heads are strong, the beer and the purses are weak. Drunkenness has also declined in the towns, partly for the same reasons, and partly because people are more sensible. Convictions for drunkenness numbered over 200,000 in 1905; in 1933 there were 36,285. The worst days of the drink-shop were in the eighteenth century, when spirits were at everybody's disposal and 'drunk for a penny, dead drunk for twopence' was the aspiration of the slums. Half a million gallons of spirits were produced in 1684; by 1714 the figure reached two millions. Government action was taken in 1736 to increase the price of gin, but there was so much illicit trading that consumption actually went up and that rapidly. Twenty million gallons of gin were drunk in England and Wales in 1742. The poor became even more sodden with gin than were the rich with port. The debauchery of the gin-drinkers was more public than that of the vinous nobility. Hogarth's *Gin Lane* depicted what everyone could see; the nightly procession of four footmen with a stretcher to remove the eleventh Duke of Norfolk from his dining-table was a private spectacle.

There is no space in which to record the various measures of reform applied during the last two centuries to make England more sober, if less free. That the old ugly habits can recur when there is a combination of good wages and bad housing was shown during the war in some munition areas, notably in the Carlisle district, which had received an enormous influx of well-paid workers for the huge war-material factories of Gretna Green. One result of this particular problem was the institution of State trading in this region; the public-houses were reduced in number and put under public control with the strict condition that the publican, now a public servant, had nothing to gain personally by the amount of alcohol he could sell. The Carlisle system was continued after the war and received a good deal of authoritative approval. In most areas, however, the combination of reduced hours of sale with the high prices consequent upon high taxation of alcohol has been effective in checking the evils of wild drinking. The Scottish habit of following neat whisky with a 'chaser' of beer has made the Scottish drink-problem in urban areas more difficult, and the Glasgow magistrates found it necessary to close the public-houses at midday on Saturday in order that the workers might return home without disastrous incursions into the wages just drawn.

During recent years there have been several movements to improve the inn and make it more representative of general social needs. The brewing companies have been persuaded to abolish their worst premises and to build better when they built afresh. The new inns along the new motoring roads are usually well designed, clean, and spacious. They lack 'atmosphere'—novelty usually does—and they cannot compare in charm with the village inn that has endured through the centuries. But they provide food and opportunities for games. Early in this century Public-House Trust companies were formed, nationally and locally, to make good inns of poor ale-houses, to remove the profit motive from the sale of intoxicants, and to transfer that motive to the sale of food. Interest on the capital involved was limited to five per cent, all surplus funds to be administered by trustees for the benefit of the community. One particular branch of this movement, known as Trust Houses, now works independently; it has acquired over two hundred premises; some of them are the most famous of old coaching inns, such as the 'Red Lion' of Colchester and the 'White Horse' of Ipswich.

It has set up a standard of cleanliness, courtesy, and reasonable prices which has been much appreciated by middle-class travellers, who thus know what to expect in service and in charges. Some people complain about the evil of centralised buying of stores and of unified control, but in my own experience the managers of Trust Houses usually take a sensible interest in their local trade and will serve local dishes; also the wine-list is moderately priced and reasonably good.

The vice of the village inn which has come up in the world owing to the new class of motoring tourists is a kind of inefficient pretentiousness. But I suppose that the blame must be laid upon the new customer at least as much as on the foolish landlord. Quite a number would rather have good ham and eggs than a bad five-course dinner with an inaccurately Frenchified menu, disguising some watery slabs of white fish with a title usually announced as 'Supreme of Barboo'. But I strongly suspect that the villainy is not all on the inn-keeper's side; if he announced an honest cut from the joint and pudding, or ham-and-eggs and a good local cheese, there are many owners of a new-bought car who would think themselves insulted, not treated as gentle-folk, deprived of the perquisites of their recent glory. So they pay their five shillings a head and get their five petty courses of indifferent victuals and worse French. A particularly noisome new arrival is the old inn bedizened to look like a night-club, with pink lampshades on the dining-tables, a constant racket of wireless and gramophone, and a smattering of urban vulgarity over all the decoration. But again the customer must bear at least half of the guilt; the young Lochinvars of the motor-bicycle and pillion and the flashy couples who roar along the arterial roads in super-charged sports models find this kind of thing very much to their taste. This kind of thing usually flourishes at about half an hour's drive from a big town. It can easily be avoided. On the whole there are far more sense and care going into the management of English inns than there were fifteen years ago.

And so we leave the English inn, naturally changing in a period of rapid social alterations. As part of the English heritage it has been all things to all periods and all tastes, superbly beautiful and squalidly mean, a grand host of the hungry and half-frozen occupants of the stage-coach and a distressing purveyor of poor food and ver-minous accommodation. It has been restful and rackety, a gin-shop and a Gin-and-It saloon, a meeting-house for scholars and a refuge of soakers, a skittle-alley, a bowling-green, a dance-hall, and a farmer's gossiping-ground. What the English choose to make of it will depend upon themselves as well as on 'the Trade'. If we give the ill-kept our complaints and the well-kept our custom, we are doing our best to turn a mixed legacy into a finer inheritance for those who come after. The better inn demands the better patron, judicious in his support, just and firm in his criticism. So might a now sorry and bedraggled house live up to one of the loveliest of the English tavern-titles and be 'The Rose Revived'.

105 AN ANGLER ON SHAKESPEARE'S AVON AT CLEEVE PRIOR MILL

106 A MEET OF THE ATHERSTONE HUNT AT
NEWNHAM PADDOX, WARWICKSHIRE

Bernard Darwin

~~~~~~

SPORT
IN THE COUNTRY

~~~~~~

THERE are no doubt some fortunate people of any one of whom it may be said that his mind is a rich epitome of all country sports. It is they who should be writing and not one who has been too foolishly fond of a single thing done in the country to spend his soul on the others. What can I say for myself? Only that though I yield to so many in knowledge I do not easily yield in feeling the romance of country things, and that they may even be the more romantic from a certain dim and golden haze that surrounds them. The most I can attempt is to write of some of their aspects that have given me pleasure and interest, though they may differ very widely from those that appeal to others.

'How for everything there is a time and a season and then how does the glory of a thing pass from it even like the flower of the grass.' So wrote George Borrow of the splendours of the old Prize-ring, and his words might

be applied to many of the sports and pastimes that at
one time or another have excited the heart of man and
sent him into the green fields. There are waves of fashion
in sporting as in other things. A great tide of popularity surges for a while and then recedes. Sometimes it
recedes for ever, but often that which was once a roaring
flood carrying everything before it becomes either a
stream, modest by comparison but yet steadily flowing
in a recognised channel, or, if not that, then a quiet
backwater still known and frequented by a faithful
few. The Ring is gone but its more orderly and less
brutal successor, boxing, survives and flourishes. Young
ladies can no longer be described, as were my grand-
mother and her sister, as 'perfect dragonesses' at archery.
They win no more glittering bracelets as prizes nor
transfix hearts as well as targets with their arrows at
garden-parties, but archery is not dead; it has its small
and select circle of solemn grown-ups, its championships
and its great little names; it has come back from what was
almost death to settle down to a quiet regular life. Have
I not seen with my own awe-stricken eyes a regiment of
ladies in Lincoln green advancing across the lawn with
disciplined steps to pluck their arrows from the row of
targets? The same may be said of croquet. As with Mr.
Pickwick after his good dinner at the Bull at Rochester,
'like a gas lamp in the street, with the wind in the pipe,
it had exhibited for a moment an unnatural brilliancy:
then sunk so low as to be scarcely discernible'. Ultimately it came back to an equable, steady-going career.
No longer does the bell on the cage ring on every lawn

as a matter of course; people are not asked to tea and croquet, but it is sternly and seriously played as a game of almost alarmingly exact skill by its considerable band of votaries.

Now and again a pastime in its renaissance far outstrips its original glories. Thirty-four years ago Mr. A. E. T. Watson wrote, 'Lawn tennis, to use a current colloquialism, looked as if it had "come to stay", and indeed its popularity is not extinct if the number and enthusiasm of its devotees have diminished. It was fatally injured by its over-perfectness. A certain number of ardent players became so expert that the game ceased to amuse the ordinary man.' How strange do those words seem now, not merely when we consider the immense popularity of Wimbledon and its heroes and heroines, who cannot even threaten to become engaged to be married without intolerable columns on the subject, but when we see out of our train window on a Saturday afternoon every back-garden and every recreation ground full of players, and a tournament for those who play in public parks attracts thousands of entries! Lawn tennis may sink again, though there is at present certainly no sign of such a thing; it may be superseded by some entirely new pursuit not yet dreamed of. Games are liable to fluctuations of fashion that do not seem to affect in the same way the sports which are rooted in the country, because these are something more than recreations and have some other reason than the exercise of the body or the amusement of the mind. Necessity and not invention was the mother of sports. Men fished and shot because they wanted food; they hunted the fox because he robbed their hen-roosts; and the utilitarian motive, if not so strong as it was, is still there at the root of the matter.

Most of us are probably too apt to think of all sports as coeval with time itself, and there we are wrong. There has always been the chase in some form or another, and if we go back to King Alfred, who was, we are told, 'a most expert and active hunter', we go back far enough, but we must not think of him and his like as the direct predecessors of Tom Smith. It was, according to Markham, 'the stagge' who was 'the most princely and roiel chase of all chases, and the first for whom indeed this Art of Hunting was first found out'. Stag-hunting is still one of the glories of Exmoor, and, in the words of a distinguished writer, 'That the ardour of the stag is incapable of being quenched by the devotion of a lifetime will be readily admitted by those who have shared with the pleasures, excitements, and dangers of the chase.' Yet the stag 'of all beasts the goodliest statelyest and most manly' has, in the general estimation, had his noble nose put out of joint by that upstart the fox, who was not hunted on an organised scale and did not enjoy the honour of having hounds entered solely to him till the middle of the eighteenth century. Modern indeed by the side of King Alfred appear Lady Salisbury, with her dwarf foxhounds and her gorgeous servants in sky-blue, or Miss Diana Draper of the East Riding. Still, a long pedigree is not everything. The glory of fox-hunting may pass, but to-day is its time and its season and more

107 A MEET OF THE STAGHOUNDS AT DUNSTER, SOMERSET

108 VILLAGE CRICKET IN THE CHILTERNS

than any other one sport it is synonymous with the country.

'The true pleasure of hunting is known only by those who hunt from home.' So wrote the noble author of the Badminton volume, and no doubt he would have enunciated this truth even more vigorously to-day when the motor-car has come to reinforce the railroad and has made rustic pursuits more and more easily available to the dweller in cities. Sport is essentially of the country and so are games, though they have become sadly urbanized. Cricket, especially if it be described by Mr. Neville Cardus, is still a lovely leisurely country thing when played at Canterbury or Worcester. When he comes to Sheffield or his own Old Trafford he can make it with equal magic a grim business set among factory chimneys. To write of cricket under the heading of sport is to risk a reproof from the meticulous who point out that hunting and shooting and fishing are sports and that anything to do with a ball is a game or a pastime. Of course they are perfectly and superfluously right, but I mean nevertheless to risk their anger and use the term in a loose and improper sense, for if I am not to be allowed at least a village cricket match then I throw down the pen.

Yet even a village cricket match is in a way just a little saddening because it is seldom quite so glorious an institution as it once was. This is not the day when 'all hearts are with little Hambledon'. Young people in villages have such a much greater choice of things to do than they once had. They can play the once 'genteel' lawn tennis and golf, and let me say parenthetically that

the 'artisan golf' movement is one of the best and friendliest of modern times; I could write whole pages on my
village golf club and the news of it that I get as I am
being driven to the station, of fours at the long hole and
twos at the short one, and the marvellous score that
caused Young Bert's handicap to be summarily reduced.
Those interloping games are not all, for there is the
omnibus that eats up the miles and takes people to the
pictures; there is the motor-cycle with its complement
the pillion-rider.

This variety of distractions does not affect cricket alone,
but all of the comparatively few amusements that once
made up country life. And so to try to write of country
sport is almost inevitably to fall at times into a mood of
gentle melancholy, to lament departed simplicity and
departed romance. It is a mood that has not come in
only with modern times; it has persisted for a good long
while now, and there is surely no better illustration of it
to be found than in the early chapters of *Tom Brown's
Schooldays*. Let those who have not read them for years,
or have only re-read the Rugby part of that great book,
turn back to the beginning again! If there be anybody
who has not read the book at all let him instantly repair
that error! Tom Hughes could be an aggravating and
blusterous person; he does, as Joe Gargery said of his
wife, 'come the Mo-gul over us now and again', but he
could write and he had a passionate patriotism for his
own Berkshire, to which everything must be forgiven.
There are surely few more spirited and delightful bits
of writing, nor one more redolent of the country, than his

account of the 'veast' with the jingling match and the wrestling and the backsword play and the sudden and exciting appearance of the old West Country champion who had fought against Shaw the Lifeguardsman years before. Here is real country sport, when men lived from year's end to year's end immobile in their own vales under the shadow of their own hills. Backsword play is, I suppose, dead; wrestling still flourishes in certain places such as, to give an obvious instance, Grasmere; there are still three-legged races at flower-shows and 'fêtes', but the country fair, and its sports, is gone, and whether we should really have enjoyed it or not, Tom Hughes can make us weep the saddest tears for it and make us feel that we have lived a good deal too late in the world.

So we are rather apt to make ungenerous comparisons without either very clear thought or very accurate knowledge, and in no sport more than in shooting is there a greater tendency to contrast the poetical past with the prosaic and businesslike present to the latter's disadvantage. There is certainly this tendency in the case of a person such as myself who does not know much about it; even if it be restrained it has to be admitted. Squire Osbaldeston in his green coat, with his famous gun by Joe Manton, and his faithful dogs of which he was so inordinately proud, is a more romantic figure than any modern shooter of driven birds. A pheasant-shoot to-day is an interesting sight as any exhibition of skill is interesting, but it does not appeal to the looker-on who is not a shooter. We—I speak of people like myself —are apt to think without any precise reason that the shooters of old days walking up the birds were more 'sportsmanlike', and that the shooting of to-day is altogether too well organised. Yet these vague feelings of ours are founded on no process of reasoning and do not justify us in saying the sort of stupid things that often are said or written. Sometimes they are said merely by people whose kindness of heart carries them away; sometimes by the Winkles of the sporting Press. They imply that modern and highly organised shooting is in the nature of a mere slaughter at which skill counts for little. This is obvious nonsense. The fine shot of to-day needs and has as much skill and endurance as any of his predecessors, is fully as anxious to match his speed and skill and cunning against that of the animal he pursues on terms which shall be exciting and difficult and shall provide a fair match. The character of shooting has changed out of knowledge, not through any change of character in those who shoot but through a change in the nature of firearms and in the nature of the country.

Osbaldeston has been mentioned as typical of the great shots of the past, and in a memoir of him the late Sir Theodore Cook well and briefly summed up the difference between the Squire's day and our own. 'Our best shots,' he wrote, 'make their records with first-rate guns under conditions often extremely difficult; the best shots of a century gone made their records under easy conditions with very poor guns.'

The heroes of old had their flint-lock muzzle-loaders; they had black powder that obscured their vision even if they had a second barrel, and the Squire, it was said, would have scorned one. So far everything was incomparably more difficult for them. On the other hand, they had not machine-cut fields which will shelter nothing, but high thick stubble, such as is unknown to-day, and they were on their birds before the birds were aware of their coming. Those who shot under these conditions achieved the utmost that anybody can achieve in being the best of the time; they made records unbeatable because the Squire killed a hundred birds with a hundred cartridges, but to say that they were better shots than their successors is as futile as to say that they were worse. It is as idle as to compare William Beldham with Hobbs or Allan Robertson with Bobby Jones. The spirit animating these different generations is the same, though our ancestors were satisfied with less than are the modern shooters. Really heavy bags have been the order of the day for scarcely a hundred years. Yet in shooting, as in other matters, all things are relative, and I heard a keen and good shot say lately, 'If you expect to get ten brace and get twelve, that is a good day.'

'Change and decay in all around I see' is at the moment the burden of the old cricketer's song when he writes to the newspapers; but he is writing of the two-eyed stance, the excessive use of the legs, and other technical crimes not for me to discuss. As regards the game in the country there is one constant lament, namely that country-house cricket is not what it was. That is alas! true; this form of the game is in temporary, perhaps permanent, eclipse, but that is not due to baser and insurgent pastimes, nor to the laziness of young gentlemen:

it is due to hard necessity. To put up a whole eleven for a week, to entertain them royally, and not only them but young ladies to dance with them, is nowadays too expensive an amusement for many people who could once keep high festival. So many private grounds are now overgrown with hay, and the pleasantest kind of cricket if not dead is moribund.

Neither is village cricket in many places what it was. The old enthusiasm, such as Miss Mitford so delightfully described, is in many places lacking. I know one club of which the president and treasurer, an old gentleman well over seventy, used to roll the pitch himself because the young sparks of the village declined to do so. They would condescend to play if they were pressed, but they let the old gentleman do the rolling, and there are not many such old gentlemen to be found. This is not a rule, I hope; if it be, there are still plenty of exceptions to it. And so to my match which, as I said, I am wholly resolved to describe.

This match is played at one of the smallest of villages which is not a great many miles from the very home of cricket, where old John Nyren saw his own village play against All England and heard Lear and Sueter singing glees at the 'Bat and Ball'. It has less than an hundred inhabitants all told, so that it has to be reinforced by a few allies—not more than three of them—from the neighbouring small town. It has, however, great enthusiasm and a wicket of which any village would be proud, since the owner of the park has given it a ground there which is carefully tended.

109 THE COURTENAY TRACY OTTERHOUNDS AT BARFORD
ST. MARTIN, WILTSHIRE

110 AN OXFORDSHIRE KILL

III DUCK-SHOOTING ON RANWORTH BROAD, NORFOLK

112 A QUIET DAY'S ANGLING ON THE LUNE RIVER, WESTMORLAND

On every Saturday it plays a match against a neighbouring team, and if possible it has them to play on its own ground, the virtues of which have given its players a distaste for those wickets where the ball flies round your head or hits you fiercely in the ribs. This particular match, however, is against no rival village; it is a fratricidal one against the staff from the big house in the park. There are several gardeners and there is the head gardener's son, who works in an office and is the shining light of the club, a good bat and a fast bowler; he is allowed on this occasion to transfer his allegiance and play for the house. There is the chauffeur, not quite so slim or so young as he used to be, for this staff remains happily unchanged for ever and ever, but no mean player still, and reputed to have been in his day a really good bowler. There is also the under-chauffeur, who had never played cricket till he came to this place, and has so far cultivated but a single stroke: as soon as the ball leaves the bowler's hand, irrespective of where it is likely to pitch, he makes a scooping movement of his bat, which sometimes meets the ball and, whenever it does so, inevitably lofts it high into the air. There is the water-bailiff, who crouches over his bat with hands held low, and, having planted it in the block hole, is disposed to keep it there. There is his son, who is a postman and so comes under the head of a hired mercenary, a hard if rugged hitter. Neither the butler nor the footman plays, but there is the nephew of the house, who is the captain, and twelve men are produced somehow.

At about half-past two the teams are gathered, the village for the most part in spotless white flannels and the dark blue caps of the club, the staff presenting a more motley aspect, since some of them make only this one cricketing appearance every year. It is the rule of the match that when a man has made nineteen he retires; so the supreme object to be attained is to make eighteen and then hit a boundary. There are white screens of highly professional appearance and a telegraph-board; the house has won the toss and comes in to bat.

For a while all goes well. The head gardener's son, whom I once saw make a hundred on this very ground, soon gets to eighteen. He is then clean bowled—a considerable triumph for the village—but he has done nearly all he could before he goes. His father sur- passes him, not in skill but in fortune, for he makes his twenty and retires amid well-deserved applause. The chauffeur is clearly a cricketer; he makes some fine hits, and he and the head gardener, being of a similar age and rotundity, run very placidly and pleasantly between the wickets. When, however, the gardener is gone, there comes in a dashing young man, who used once to be an under-chauffeur, and he nearly runs his old master out. Fortunately he fails, and his rash enterprise produces several overthrows.

The opening pair of bowlers are both fastish and straightest and no great liberties can be taken with them, but the game cheers up wonderfully when the rector comes on as first change to bowl his leg breaks. He tosses them almost impudently high and slowly into the air, so that the spectator itches to be a player, and yet there is more in this bowling than meets the eye. If Mr. Jessop were batting I doubt if the leg breaks would greatly avail, for the ball would not often hit the pitch, but as it is he has people guessing and slogging and missing. The bat whistles ferociously through the air, but it does not always meet the ball; the chauffeur, somewhat out of breath with running short runs and nearing his nineteen, is stumped by yards, and somebody else is caught off a mis-hit, and now the tail is coming in and the bowling that began by looking so inviting seems to take on a mysterious and fiendish aspect. The young postman makes a gallant effort. He bears, as the sporting reporters say, a charmed life, for he is missed three times in four balls, and once again a little later, but the other wickets fall steadily, and 105 is justly regarded as a respectable score.

Alas! it is not big enough. The first pair of village batsmen look so businesslike that it seems that they will be like Dumkins and Podder of All-Muggleton and make fifty runs before they are parted. However, misfortune comes to them both: the gardener's son can now and again bowl a ball that would make anybody think. A left-handed ally from the town makes as fine a hit into the neighbouring hay as anyone could wish to see; it goes 'sailing with supreme dominion' high over the screen and it is the general view that it would have pitched into the pavilion at Lord's. He tries incontinently to do it again and is clean bowled next ball. One way or another some five wickets are down for seventy runs and the young postman is making an ungenerous return for being missed four times by catching everything that comes to him. The village is sure to have a tail, and anything may happen. At this most inopportune moment the chauffeur is put on to bowl. He does look like a good bowler but he starts by bowling to leg, and there is a batsman, with a two-eyed stance, who is impotent on the off side but can hit to leg. Bang, bang, bang, bang—there are four boundaries in less than no time; the match is as good as over and in the end the village win easily enough, but if only one more wicket could have fallen at that crucial moment. . . . Well, well, it is idle to repine, and the house bears up wonderfully.

After the match comes the crowning glory of the day, the supper. The squash-rackets court at the house is adorned with Union Jacks and filled with trestle tables. There are the two teams and the house's owner, who is the president of the club, and one or two people who are staying with him. There is roast beef and roast mutton, plum pudding and bread and cheese; there is lots of beer, and when the cloth is taken off and it is time to drink healths there is rum punch so hot that the glass nearly burns your fingers. It does not need a great effort of the imagination to fancy yourself at Hambledon.

There is at first an inclination to silence but it soon disappears before the beer and the hospitable ways and there is a general and cheerful buzzing long before the King's health is drunk. After that the president proposes the club and the rector replies, chaffing the staff gently on the fact that some of them are a little older and balder and fatter than they used to be, because they all stay so long in their places, whereas the village team has young blood. That gives a great opportunity for the staff when it comes to their turn to reply to the toast of their health, and the gardener declares that he has been there for twenty something years and does not want to be turned out just yet, and the butler, who has been largely responsible for the smooth running of the supper, follows on the same lines. The president, being the founder of the feast as well, has naturally to make several speeches, and then comes the singing.

The gardener is called on first and he sings 'Cock Robin' in a very pleasant voice. It takes some time because there are a good many verses and after each verse the singer first proclaims alone that 'All the birds of the air went a-sighing and a-sobbing' and then all the room proclaims it with him. Each singer has the right to call on another, and hands on the song-book to him. So the gardener calls on the rector and the rector, having done his duty most nobly, calls on another gardener who passes it on to a cowman, and so on. There is 'John Peel' and there is 'Bring back my Bonny' and there is a delightful song in a narrative form called 'The Old Arm-chair'. Granny dies, and when it comes to the reading of the will she is found to have left the singer, who does not conceal his disappointment, nothing but the old arm-chair:

> How they tittered, how they chaffed,
> How my brothers and my sisters laughed.

But the laugh turned against them, for presently the

chair fell to pieces with long usage and hidden in the seat was discovered five thousand pounds.

This song has been sung regularly and received rapturously year after year. A perceptible thrill of anticipation runs through the company as the singer rises to his feet, but there is an even greater one when the water-bailiff supposes that they would like the old song again and bursts into a ballad in which he sings the girl's verses in falsetto and then responds as her lover with ferocious gruffness. The president has two songs and there is a pleasing state of uncertainty as to which he will sing. This year he chooses 'I married a wife and then, I married a wife and then' and is loudly cheered. One of his guests sings 'John Brown's body'—rather too high—and the other, being unable even to do even so much, tells one or two mild stories which are kindly received. The butler gives another hardy annual, a recitation about nick-nacks, and the knock-kneed knocker-up, to which 'Sister Susie sewing shirts for soldiers' is the simplest thing in the world, and how he can remember it from one year to another nobody knows. Then soon after ten o'clock the house retires amid 'He's a jolly good fellow'; the rector goes too, the gardener moves into the chair and the singing goes on till all the beer and all the rum punch are finished. This calamity, judging by sounds of 'Auld Lang Syne' and 'God Save the King', does not befall till hard on midnight, and everybody goes soberly and gratefully home just before the Sunday morning breaks. It has been a great day—country cricket at its best and in the friendliest of all possible places. 'If any of the old

English yeomen had turned into fairies when they died it is just the place in which they would have held their revels.'

I have put in my cricket, I fear, at inordinate length because I love it best. I have also no doubt put it in out of its turn. Fox-hunting ought by prescriptive right to have come first. Shooting has changed out of knowledge because it demands a mechanical instrument and that has changed out of knowledge too. Hunting demands no mechanism but men, horses, and foxes, and they remain more or less constant. So it has been said that if the immortal Squire or his contemporaries were to come back to the Shires from some Elysian gorse or pastures they would know where they were; they would be astonished at the numbers of the field, but they would have nothing to learn. The hunting would be in essentials the hunting they knew. It would not be with them as it was with the great Mr. Meynell, who in his own lifetime saw the sport so changed by the new school of hard riders that he never knew a happy moment afterwards.

There is still for its devotees no other pursuit so absorbing, which so wholly pervades their lives so that they become a race set apart, alarming and mysterious to those who do not share their interests, at once the envy and the jest of the pedestrian world. Once, a good many years ago, I stayed in a small hotel at St. Andrews with a gentleman whom I never chanced to see upon the links. Yet every night at dinner he joined so easily and pleasantly, if unobtrusively, in the conversation that I had no thought but that he was a golfer. It was only at the end of my stay that I discovered from his own lips that he had never played. That was a wonderful achievement on his part, for golfers talk plenty of 'shop', but could he have done the same thing among hunting men at Melton? I think that would have been too much for him.

Horses, it has recently been observed by a sardonic author, are the one subject on which stupid men can be clever. They are also certainly a subject, though not the only one, on which otherwise reasonably intelligent people can be stupid. Yet, even to those of us who are thus stupid, hunting can possess one attraction of its own which to the genuinely horsy will perhaps be incomprehensible. There are, I know, many people who never hunt, and to whom the whole art and mystery are as a sealed book, and yet they look regularly at the hunting news in their *Times* on a winter morning. They do so because of the irresistible attraction of the names of the villages, the spinneys, the gorses. It may be said that they could enjoy the same sensations from reading an Ordnance Survey Map, and that indeed is far from being without its glow, for there is scarce a field in England that has not got a good name of its own, if we can but find it out. It is, however, the hunting that wraps the names in their peculiar glory and romance. Is there not some strange magic in Thrussington Gorse, Wartnaby Stonepits, and Brentingby Spinneys? To the hunting man they are real places full of real and exciting memories; to us who only read of them they are beautiful for their own sakes. I can read pages of Dick Christian's lectures for the names in them. Listen to his account of a famous

234

113 GUNS MOVING TO A NEW DRIVE AT WESTWOOD PARK,
WORCESTERSHIRE

114 THE END OF A DAY WITH THE BLEAN BEAGLES, KENT

115 A DAY'S SHOOTING AT ENDERBY, LEICESTERSHIRE

run with the Cottesmore. 'We found at Armley Wood, then through Empingham, Cottesmore Wood, straight through Exton Park, across the North Road by Horn Lane toll-bar, through Ardwick Wood, where the balloon from Nottingham fell, The Lings, Fowthorpe Oaks, Stamford Field-side, Royal Belthorpe, Rasen Gretford; then we came to Langtoft and Deeping—let me see— and Tallerton, and then by Uppington Wood, and killed at Essendine Park—that's it.' That's it indeed, and the same joy, on a smaller scale, can be had for twopence, if we know the right day to look for it, all through the winter.

Perhaps we enjoy these names of places the more because we are somewhat starved in names of living men. Modern games give full play to the hero-worshipping instinct in man, and the names of some great hero of the ball sound stirring in the ears of thousands who have scarcely beheld him. There are doubtless personages as great in the hunting-field, but the man in the street has never heard of them because there is to-day no one to tell him about them. They lack the poet who shall celebrate them. Nimrod and the Druid told the world of famous men of their time, and 'still are their pleasant voices, their nightingales awake'. We still know not only about Tom Smith and the Squire and Dick Christian, but about Holyoake and Maher, Sir Bellingham Graham and Sir Richard Sutton, and Mr. Greene of Rolleston, who became immortal in a single sentence because he skimmed over the Whissendine 'like a swallow on a summer evening'. It may be a cheap instinct in us that makes us look for some hero of notoriety, for some great 'personalities'. It may be that we are debased by the modern newspaper, with its intensely personal note. At any rate, for better or for worse the mighty hunters of to-day enjoy, as regards the great heart of the public, a private and anonymous glory. They are known in their own counties and in their own circles, and the rest of the world knows them not. This is doubtless a good thing; it keeps a sport unvulgarised; it makes fame a secondary object to the sport itself. My only complaint is that it deprives me personally of good and exciting reading that I should enjoy if there were anyone good enough to write it. I cannot help wishing for someone to tell me who to-day is 'the mightiest hunter that ever rode across Belvoir's sweet vale with a horn at his saddle-bow'. Is there no one now great enough to say 'There never again shall be such a Mr. Smith as long as the world stands'?

It is part of this pleasant privacy of hunting that it has no deliberate gallery of spectators. We who are on the road may chance to encounter a horseman or two jogging along to or from a meet; we may, if we are lucky, look over a hedge and catch a fleeting glance of the hunt. If we live in a hunting country we may go to a meet. Nobody can buy a seat in a grandstand to see a hunt, and the same is true of shooting or fishing. As we walk by a river we catch sight of a fisherman, but to stand and watch him would make us feel obtrusive and uncomfortable. We should be as the little boys who crowd round an unhappy landscape-painter and look over his shoulder. There is something indecent and ill-mannered

in encroaching ever so slightly on that absorbed tranquillity. We pause and look at a game of cricket or football and think no shame to do so; nay, we are paying the
players the highest compliment we can in offering them a
gallery, but we should not look over a wall at a game of
lawn tennis in a garden. There is a difference of some sort;
the cricketer on a village green offers himself as a spectacle, but the sportsman seems always, metaphorically, to
be in his own garden.

Now and again he emerges into the full glare of the
public eye. The point-to-point meeting, for instance,
is essentially a public festival. Here the hunting folk
openly offer themselves to be looked at, and even in the
least hunting of counties all the world is ready to come
to see them. In my own almost suburban county, though
it is an insult to call anything so lovable by such an
epithet, we found ourselves blocked and crawling at
a foot's pace for half an hour at least along a road that
led to a point-to-point. How much of all that crowd was
due to the innate desire to have something on a horse,
how much to be in the swim of what was going forward,
how much to see a jolly sight in a pretty place on a fine
day, and how much to a genuine interest in the horses
and the racing it is impossible to say. At any rate, there
it was with its ring of bookmakers and its farm-carts
making stands for the neighbourhood, and its women
wheeling their babies, and its itinerant singers, singing
the same two melancholy songs and pursuing us round
and round the clump of trees that were the vantage-point.
And this in Kent, only twenty-something miles from

London, where the daily-breader daily leaves his home in the morning with his season-ticket and his umbrella and comes back at night with his evening paper. The years seemed to have rolled away and it was still genuine country after all.

It is, I think, the privacy and placidity of fishing that appeal to the man who is not an enthusiast for the sport's own sake. That appeal becomes the more poignant perhaps as he grows older and less violently active, and, to make an egotistical remark, I often and often wish that I had taken my chances when I was young. Everybody had not the opportunities of hunting or shooting, but I might have become some sort of a fisherman. In the little house on the hill in Wales where I spent many summer holidays the veranda floor still reproaches me, when I see it, with wasted chances. On its rough slates are cut the images of the fish once brought home then in triumph from the Dovey or the Dulas, with the initials of the happy conqueror. The Dovey ran almost at the drive gate; at the top of the hill, whither one climbed by the rocky path through the groves of stunted oaks, there was a lake, and in the lake were a few trout. I might at any rate have tried to learn there, but golf had me too fast in its grip; I grudged any day that was spent away from the links, and day after day a train—and generally a very late train—bore me away to Aberdovey.

I feel most conscious of this misspent youth when I stay in a pleasant house in Hampshire and five minutes' walk takes me down to the banks of the Itchen. There is the old stone bridge crossing it where one can lean on the balustrade and mesmerise oneself by looking into the shallow stream so intensely clear. And on either hand are tall, green reeds and—I think—willow herb and loosestrife. Beyond the bridge is the old mill, with roses clustering on it, now a mill no longer, but still having its pool and its rushing water. There is not a soul in sight save one figure wading in the stream. I, in my innocence, can see no hope of his catching anything, but my guide can see the brown shadowy form lurking by a stone or at the edge of the reeds, and presently I, in mortal fear of making too much sound or of committing some nameless wickedness that I know not of, see or think I can see it too. I can only dimly appreciate the fisherman's skill, though I do know that, were I to try, my line would be instantly in the saddest tangle; I do not fully understand either his hopes or his disappointments, but I feel for a moment or two a pathetic yearning and think that in such a spot dry-fly fishing must bring man nearer to heaven than any other amusement in the world.

> Sometimes too early and sometimes too late,
> Sometimes too little and sometimes in spate;
> Sometimes too windy and sometimes too calm,
> Sometimes too frosty and sometimes too warm;
> Sometimes too drumlie and sometimes too clear
> There's aye something wanting when I'm fishing here.

That side of the fisherman's life, so touchingly set forth, is no doubt one that I do not fully appreciate as I repose by the banks of the Itchen. It has been in a sense ameliorated by telegrams and the telephone, the train and the motor-car, for the fisherman can learn in an instant whether the conditions are favourable before he sets out, or, when they are not, he can go home to his business or to some other and inferior pleasure, and return when he hears that things have taken a turn for the better. In earlier days it was not so; the fisherman laid his plans, he went to the appointed spot and had to make the best of things. The annals of the famous Houghton Club at Stockbridge bear witness to this change. In the old books are all manner of charades and *jeux d'esprit*, English verses, and even Latin elegiacs. The modern ones contain only a dry and businesslike record of achievement.

The salmon fisherman, who has to go much further afield, may, for aught I know, write his verses still when the gods are unkind to him; and the dry-fly fisherman can at any rate still give vent to his feelings in charming prose. It would be difficult to find a piece of writing more full of the true feeling of the countryman and the fisherman than Lord Grey of Fallodon's description of dashing from London to the delights of a Hampshire stream. The longing beforehand, the sudden resentment against the town, the early walk over Waterloo Bridge, are all lovingly dwelt upon and then 'At some time between eight and nine o'clock you step out of the train, and are in a few minutes amongst all the long-desired things. Every sense is alert and excited, every scent and everything seen or heard is noted with delight. You are grateful for the grass on which you walk, even for the soft country dust about your feet.' If those words can speak so eloquently to the layman what must they mean to the fisherman! *'Ecoutez les Gascons—c'est toute la Gascogne.'*

I am painfully conscious that there are sports of which I have not even attempted to say anything—stalking, for instance, of which I know no more than can be learnt from John Leech's divine pictures of Mr. Briggs in old bound volumes of Mr. Punch. There is otter-hunting too, and beagling—but I grow overwhelmed. There is one country amusement on which I will add a word or two. It is one in which nearly all of us are onlookers rather than doers, namely the sheep-dog trial. It has lately become more widely known than ever before since some of the most illustrious dogs have performed their wonders in Hyde Park, but there is something insulting and almost indecent in bringing them there. I can only think of them when I have seen them in Wales.

The trial is held in a big meadow on a steeply sloping hill-side above the little town; we look down on the shining waters of the estuary and the great sandhills beyond them and so out to sea. The spectators are scattered under the lee of the surrounding hedges, some above and some below, but the officials and dogs and their masters are collected at the lower end of the field, and there is the pen into which the sheep have to be driven. The sheep come in from a gate at the top of the field, and then at his master's signal the dog is up the slope after them. Sometimes he dashes swiftly, sometimes he creeps stealthily, and his master from below talks to him in mysteriously modulated whistles and signs. There are sets of posts, as it were goal-posts, through which the sheep have to be driven, and the cunning dog herds them to the very mouth of the goal by stages, waiting each time for the word of command, and the rash young dog is impetuous and tries to do too much at once. Even for the casual spectator there are so many moments of dreadful agony, of overflowing sympathy. He would like to kill that fool of a sheep that spoils everything just in the hour of victory, and cannot emulate the patience either of the dog or the master, who only settle down with such good-humour to repair the mischief. The last agony is the greatest when the actual penning is to be done and the master himself is allowed to take a hand with the dog. Two sheep are safely in but one is obdurate, and when every second is of importance the whole weary work has to be begun over again. It is almost too much for human flesh and blood. It gives the same intolerable sensation as waiting for the start of a hundred-yards race, when the men are inclined to break away and there has already been a false start or two, so that at last we shut our eyes and wait for the sound of the pistol. The sight of that last sheep is more than can be endured, especially if the shepherd is old and the dog young and inexperienced so that each of them wrings our heartstrings for opposite reasons. It is an unspeakable relief when the task is accomplished and the master gives the servant a brief and never fulsome word of approval.

For my part I find the actual competition almost too agonising, and enjoy better the exhibition that comes afterwards, for the thrill is as great and the suffering less keen. Here is the great Mr. H, the pride of Merioneth, who is going to show how it should be done, first with two dogs simultaneously and then with three. Each of the dogs has a name which is known far and wide; I am ashamed to say I have now forgotten them, though at the time I whispered them with worshipping awe. Here surely is the most perfect example of team-work that any game has to show, each dog doing his part as a piece of a machine and yet each being so intensely human with a character of his own. Two of them are old and have been showing themselves for years to their admirers; one is young, bred up to follow in their footsteps, a knight who has only just won his spurs, already worthy of his company but still lacking something of his elders' machine-like accuracy. Once, just once, he makes ever so slight a slip, and we feel that the other two must be thinking pityingly of his youth. The supreme moment comes when two of the three take their places as living goal-posts and the third drives the sheep between them. This is the high and heroic state of dogs.

Thank goodness nobody agrees to-day with Laven-gro's acquaintance, Joey, who thought there was nothing like dog-fighting. 'A time will come', he said, 'when folks will give up everything else and follow a dog-fighting.' Fortunately he was a bad prophet, and over the decadence of some country sports there is no need to grow sentimental. If cocking is not yet quite dead few people, even if they know where to look for it, want to see a main. That it can be seen by those to whom 'the office' is given, there is little doubt; indeed there were some public court proceedings about a cock-fight not long ago. Mr. Wentworth Day, an amateur in such matters who knows his East Anglia well, has some interesting remarks on the subject in his book *A Falcon on St. Paul's*. He declares that within the last four or five years a main of cocks was fought at Hampstead, and that cocking may be seen at Newmarket, near Norwich and near Doncaster, in Nottinghamshire and the Welsh Marches, and in Northumberland villages; further, that he thinks he could name a little public-house in Romford, where at intervals the knowing ones could find what they want. It may well be so, but not only has cocking been illegal for nearly a hundred years but public opinion has definitely set against it for fully as long a time. It has become a secret and squalid business, much as did prize-fighting when the great days of the ring were over. Once a thing has to be done shame-facedly and under the rose, with spies set out to see lest there be 'hawks abroad', its days are numbered, and in this case at least nobody can pretend to regret it. In one of the most engaging gardens in Wales there still stands an ancient cock-pit, the only one of my acquaintance. It is quite close to the house, and it is easy to imagine the gentlemen carrying out their port wine with them across the grass. I like to think that a little silver cup which a Welsh ancestor of mine won in a cock-fight records a triumph in that very pit. To-day it is half overgrown with brambles, some of the stones in its circular wall have fallen out, and there is grass growing through the floor. It stands there, neglected, a *memento mori*, a sign that 'for all things there is a time and a season'.

244

INDEX

(The numerals in italic denote the *figure numbers* of the illustrations)

245